# PRAISE FOR
## *The New Human Capital Strategy*

"Hall has put it all together in this insightful and highly constructive book. As both an academic and senior HR executive, his unique perspectives on human resource management has resulted in a groundbreaking and integrative approach to human resource management. While we can all appreciate that people are the key to competitive advantage, Hall's key contribution is his development of a comprehensive and integrated model for human capital. This is sorely needed, especially today when HR professionals are seeking new ways to get traction in their companies. This book is not only thoroughly researched, but brilliantly written. A must-read for everyone who takes leadership development seriously."

—Allen Morrison, Ph.D., Professor,
Global Management and IMD, Lausanne, Switzerland

"Nothing sparkles on the shelf like a management book that explains complex issues with simple insight. *The New Human Capital Strategy* provides a compelling theory of people management for sustained business performance. But its real value lies in its powerful pragmatism. Hall's book is destined to become a diamond in the rough of human resource theory."

—Michael Dixon, Ph.D., Vice President,
Global Business Services, IBM Asia Pacific Melbourne, Australia

"A real breakthrough in approaching this subject from a practical angle. This is neither a 'nice to read' philosophical essay of little use nor a standard 'how to' book. Brad Hall takes the human dimension of organizations to a new strategic level. By placing human capital in a business context bringing together the internal and external environment, he provides organizations with a true opportunity to finally meet the challenge of making 'people their greatest asset.' His practical roadmap gives a meaningful perspective allowing people to make a greater contribution to the strategic growth of their organization by discovering their true potential."

—Jean Claude Noel, Program Director, INSEAD Global Leadership Center; and former COO of Christie's International—Paris, France

*(more . . .)*

# THE NEW
# HUMAN
# CAPITAL
# STRATEGY

### Improving the Value of Your
### Most Important Investment—Year after Year

## Bradley W. Hall, Ph.D.

**American Management Association**
New York • Atlanta • Brussels • Chicago • Mexico City • San Francisco
Shanghai • Tokyo • Toronto • Washington, D.C.

Special discounts on bulk quantities of AMACOM books are available to corporations, professional associations, and other organizations. For details, contact Special Sales Department, AMACOM, a division of American Management Association, 1601 Broadway, New York, NY 10019.
Tel.: 212-903-8316.   Fax: 212-903-8083.
Web Site: www.amacombooks.org

This publication is designed to provide accurate and authoritative information in regard to the subject matter covered. It is sold with the understanding that the publisher is not engaged in rendering legal, accounting, or other professional service. If legal advice or other expert assistance is required, the services of a competent professional person should be sought.

Library of Congress Cataloging-in-Publication Data

Hall, Bradley W.
    The new human capital strategy : improving the value of your most important investment—year after year / Bradley W. Hall.
        p.   cm.
    Includes bibliographical references and index.
    ISBN-13: 978-0-8144-0927-5
    ISBN-10: 0-8144-0927-X
    1. Human capital—Management.   2. Performance—Evaluation.
    3. Personnel management—Evaluation.   4. Organizational effectiveness—
    Evaluation.   5. Corporations—Valuation.   I. Title.
    HD4904.7.H285   2008
    658.3'01—dc22

                                                            2007024945

Printing number

10   9   8   7   6   5   4   3   2   1

# Contents

## PART 2: BUILDING THE SYSTEM

# Foreword

Have you ever thought, after reading something, "That makes so much sense! Why didn't *I* think of this before?" In my experience, this is the hallmark of almost every path-breaking book. Its author somehow is able to examine in a fresh or different light, a problem that has vexed us for a very long time, exposing the flaws in how we previously had framed the problem so that the solution becomes clear.

This was my experience when I read an early draft of Brad Hall's book, *The New Human Capital Strategy*. Brad points out a number of ironies in the way most of us manage our people that, once he has pointed them out, seem at best nonsensical—just filled with contradictions. A platitude of management is that people are every organization's most important asset, for example. And yet most organizations' processes for building and cultivating those critically important assets are not processes at all. They are programs, which are conceived episodically, opportunistically, or reactively. Then, to compound the problem, most of our organizations have no way to measure the results of our efforts to build their people. We measure the *activities* and the *spending* that are *inputs* toward that purpose. But we don't measure—and in many ways *can't* measure—their effectiveness or the results.

Another example: There is powerful evidence from scholars such as Frederick Herzberg that the primary motivators for managers are opportunities to grow, to achieve and learn, to be an important and recognized player on a team, and to make a difference in an important cause. These are the factors that create within us an intrinsic willingness to work and sacrifice for the good of the organization that gives us those opportunities. These researchers have shown that financial compensation is, at best, a *hygiene* factor. It's important not to mess compensation up, because inequities in compensation create disgruntlement. But financial incentives don't create that deep willingness to sacrifice for the good of the organization. In the face of that evidence, isn't it interesting how many executives are obsessed with designing bullet-proof incentive compensation schemes? It is as if their hope is to embed within a compensation formula a carrot here, a nudge there, and a kick in the rear end on occasion, so that the people thereby incentivized don't need to be managed. So many "managers" want to abdicate to a formula those things that are the essence of management—creating opportunities for our people to succeed at important, challenging responsibilities.

Here's a third illustration. We bemoan the short pay-off horizons of many executives when considering investments to create new growth products and businesses. We assert that companies would be much stronger if only executives could take a longer view—and we blame the demands of financial markets for truncating managerial vision at the end of the current quarter. Then we turn around, however, and create for the most promising of the future leaders of our companies career paths that entail moving from one responsibility to the next every two years. In many ways the blame for our inability to invest for the long term ought not be laid at the feet of Wall Street analysts. Rather, the cause is rooted in our management development processes, wherein we penalize the careers of aspiring managers if they expend resources on initiatives that can't pay off during their two-year watch in a given position. We espouse one virtue, and then disavow it in practice.

Most managers of manufacturing organizations simply would not tolerate reject rates of five percent coming off the end of their manufacturing lines. They'd work nights and weekends, bring in legions of six-sigma black-belt engineers and trainers, and do almost anything else that was required to make their processes so capable that they could make perfect products every time. The managers of those same companies will also say that getting the right people in the right jobs at the right time is their most important responsibility. And yet the processes of hiring and promoting the people with the skills required to succeed in critical jobs suffer from rejection rates as high as 20 percent in many of these same companies. How can we be so complacent, when the process that we all say is the most crucial is out of control?

One of the greatest ironies of management is that the processes of building and utilizing our organizations' most important resources in the most productive and effective way possible is probably the least understood of all of the dimensions of management. And it is not understood because it has rarely been studied in rigorous ways by those of us who should be studying it. This is why I'm so delighted to see Brad's book, *The New Human Capital Strategy*. It is a pioneering book in a field that needs pioneers who have the discipline for rigorous thought. Like all pioneers, Brad Hall can't begin to cover the whole territory in a single effort. While I hope that Brad's work will be directly helpful to those who read this book, my more important hope is that it will provide a framework within which other scholars can contribute to the resolution of so many of these contradictions that characterize the way we manage our people.

—Clayton Christensen, Harvard Business School

# THE NEW

# HUMAN

# CAPITAL

# STRATEGY

# A Systematic Approach to Growing Your Human Capital

*"Innovation in management principles and processes can create long-lasting advantage and produce dramatic shifts in competitive position. Over the past 100 years, management innovation, more than any other kind of innovation, has allowed companies to cross new performance thresholds."*

*—GARY HAMEL, 2006*[1]

We often hear that people are the most important variable for an organization's success. Yet do you know of a single corporation that can confidently state that its human assets are more valuable this year than last? How would one measure that?

Business leaders are similarly regarded as critical to business success. A quick search on Amazon.com delivers more than 194,000 books on leadership, so it must be important. Yet do you know of an organization that knows whether its leaders are better this year than last? What is "better" anyway?

In your organization, over the past twelve months, which human resources programs and activities (e.g., stock options, employee appraisals) created measurable value to customers or shareholders? Can't say? Here's an easier question: Of all those programs and activities, which added customer or shareholder value?

Still struggling? Let's make the question even easier by removing customers and shareholders from the equation: In the past twelve months, which people improvement activities delivered the expected results? Think of your performance appraisal cycle, sales rep training, or employee satisfaction improvement program and ask: "Did it work?" If the performance appraisal cycle is designed to improve alignment, motivation, and productivity, does that happen? Does sales training improve rep performance in the eyes of their customers? Have employee satisfaction initiatives improved employee satisfaction ratings?

Notice how these questions are tied to business results rather than to activities or program deliverables. However, more often than not in today's business world, the goal is to deliver world-class programs rather than world-class people. All too frequently, companies wind up with volumes of programs and activities, few of which produce real results for employees, customers, or shareholders. In your company, are people-related programs and activities designed to deliver results to a well-conceived blueprint of a high-performing organization, or are they simply efforts to demonstrate that management cares? It is difficult to imagine plumbers, electricians, and roofers diligently working without a blueprint of the finished product, but we do it all the time with human capital programs.

Think about your company. Perhaps your senior leaders talk about people being the most important variable for business success. If so, do the leaders have a vision of success, how it connects to business results, and how to systematically grow it over time? And who is accountable for delivering that vision? If you don't have an end-state blueprint of human capital, and there is no owner, you certainly cannot manage *it* for success.

Perhaps this explains the 2006 finding by the University of Southern California (USC)'s Center for Effective Organizations that only 9 percent of HR leaders report that their company is effective or very effective in connecting human capital practices to organizational performance.[2] That leaves 91 percent who do not believe that their human capital practices effectively connect with organizational performance—a pretty tough self-assessment.

How is it that a company's most important variable is so loosely managed? Let's compare today's human capital management model to the manufacturing profession. It's difficult to imagine the head of manufacturing for an industrial company meeting with the CEO at year end and saying: "We're not really sure whether our manufacturing capabilities improved since last year. In fact, we really don't know how to define manufacturing excellence. So unfortunately, I cannot report whether last year's initiatives and investments improved our manufacturing capabilities."

Of course, this would never happen in manufacturing. Manufacturing leaders have clearly defined outputs; and those outputs matter to customers and shareholders. Manufacturing leaders build a system to deliver the expected outputs and use metrics to understand the contribution of each subsystem. Manufacturing leaders have to manage with discipline because so much financial capital is tied up in plants. Now look at the financial capital invested in salaries. Employee pay is the biggest line-item expense for many companies. For bottom-line financial performance, effective management of human capital should be as important to customers and shareholders as the effective management of manufacturing.

## Time for a New Approach

It is time for a new, systemic approach to growing human capital. This is an approach: (1) that clearly describes what successful human capital is and how it connects to business results, (2) that measures and manages human capital with the same discipline as financial capital, and (3) that enables company managers to learn from experience to make progressively better human capital decisions. It is time for Human Capital Management (HCM)—a system designed to create sustained competitive advantage through people.

THE THEORY OF HUMAN CAPITAL MANAGEMENT

Human Capital Management holds that business profits are generated and sustained when a company provides products and services
that meet customers' needs better than competitors do—in other
words, when the company has a competitive advantage. Businesses create and maintain that advantage over time when their
core competencies, or the activities that customers value most, are
superior to those of their competitors in the eyes of their current
and potential customers.[3] *Human Capital Management is a system
for improving the performance of those in critical roles*—those with
the biggest impact on corporate core competencies.

Not all roles in a company are equally important for customer and
shareholder satisfaction. Industry-best sales reps, for example, create
more customer and shareholder value than industry-best administrative assistants. In the HCM model, the question "Are our people better than our competitors' people?" may be more accurately stated as:
"Is the performance of those in critical roles superior to those of peers
in competitor organizations?" The answer is often knowable.

What does HCM success look like? Success is when a company
can state that "our people outperform competitors' people" in roles
that add the most value to customers and shareholders. Success is not
world-class talent; it is world-class performance.

If performance improvement of those in critical roles is the goal,
then all human capital programs, tools, activities, and even meetings
must be evaluated by their impact on making "our people better than
the competitors' people." For example, if there are four things that big
deal makers need to do well to sell big deals, then all programs and developmental activities for deal makers should be focused on driving
performance improvements on those four things. In addition to a focused development effort, an effective HCM system requires a data-
rich, analytic approach to measuring and managing human capital
with the same discipline as financial capital. Certainly, behavior is not
as easily measured as financial results, but it definitely can be meas-

ured. As a graduate student in psychology, I read a study that showed human fetuses prefer music with human voices to instrumental music. "How can they know that?" I wondered. The answer is reached by triangulating galvanic skin response, blood pressure, and heart rate, and comparing that with children and adults. If researchers can figure that out, we certainly ought to be able to measure workplace behavior and performance. Measuring human behavior and performance *is* possible. It's just not being effectively done in most corporations today.

Some might say that measuring and managing people devalues the worth of human beings. I disagree. In fact, I believe that for several reasons, it is a disservice to *not* measure people and performance. The first reason is that people want to know they are successful. Make people successful, and they will be happy. Think about a room with ten sales reps, nine of whom are not making quota. Will free soft drinks or movie nights make the reps happy? Probably not. The way to make them happy is to make them successful. The primary purpose of HCM is to make external customers and shareholders happy—not to make internal customers (such as employees) happy. Employees will be satisfied only when they see that their work makes a meaningful contribution to the business. And that requires a system that measures, develops, and celebrates their contributions.

The second reason it is a disservice not to measure people's performance is that activity without feedback is no fun. Think about it: How many people would continue to bowl if they had to wear a blindfold? The only reason that throwing a heavy ball is fun is that bowlers get immediate feedback, make adjustments, and try again. Human beings love a good challenge. Human beings like to win.

The third reason is that when performance is not objectively measured, politics fill the gap. Think of yourself as an assistant professor trying to get tenure. In a system with unclear measures, getting tenure requires ingratiating yourself with faculty power brokers. You are at the mercy of the judgments of others, some of whom see you as a threat. A wise strategy is to play conservatively and not rock the boat. A clearly defined set of standards shifts the power from the faculty committee to the assistant professor.

It is rarely beneficial to a company or its people when politics fill a performance measurement gap. Several years ago, when I was helping a

Japanese company start up a new training organization, I went back to the United States for a week. I phoned to leave a voicemail message for a team member and was surprised when she picked up the phone at 8:30 P.M. Tokyo time. I said, "Sato san, why are you still at work?" She said, "I am very busy!" I said, "Busy doing what? We haven't started up yet." She replied, "Oh, I am very busy." She was actually busy looking busy. With no objective performance measures, employees were evaluated by their diligence, not by their results—and employees stayed late into the night to demonstrate that diligence. If you truly care about your people, then measure, manage, and celebrate their results.

## Today's Approach to Human Capital Management

Today's approach for improving workforce performance is failing. There are three reasons:

1.  No one is accountable for year-over-year human capital performance.
2.  Results require a system, not world-class programs.
3.  Today's HR model is misaligned to deliver business results.

Let's look at each of these reasons.

### No One Is Accountable

The head of manufacturing is accountable for year-over-year improvements in manufacturing productivity. The head of marketing is accountable for year-over-year changes in brand equity. The head of sales is responsible for revenue growth. But who is responsible for year-over-year improvements in the company's most valuable asset—its people? Nobody. Line managers see HR as accountable, but HR sees itself accountable for programs that must be converted into business results by line managers. No one is in charge of human capital performance.

### Systems, Not Programs

The HR profession is very adept at program development. Success is most often defined as creating and/or adopting best-practice programs, and HR is organized and managed accordingly. HR consulting firms align their practices with the way their clients are organized: They deliver products and programs for HR subprofessions (such as training, staffing, and compensation). But the data is indisputable: Decades of new and better programs have not delivered great results. The reason is that "world-class programs" cannot deliver performance results. Only systems deliver results.

An automobile engine is a system that requires great parts. All parts must be fully integrated and aligned to the purpose of the engine, whether that be high performance or a fuel economy. A well-built engine uses just the right parts and no more. Likewise, succession planning, training, and appraisal can be viewed as parts. Just as throwing pistons and spark plugs into an engine compartment will not deliver a satisfactory engine, neither will "world-class" HR programs deliver acceptable customer results. More and better HR programs will deliver no better performance in the future than they have in the past. Performance results require a system.

## A Misaligned Model

There is plentiful data demonstrating that HR is not delivering to expectations. *The Economist*'s "2006 CEO Briefing" cited HR as tied for the least important corporate function, the worst performing of all corporate functions, and second to last in importance for achieving business results for the next three years.[4] In addition, the consulting company Accenture's 2006 High Performance Workforce study found that only 5 percent of CEOs and 4 percent of CFOs are very satisfied with their human resource function.[5] The same study indicated that 3 percent of CEOs and 4 percent of CFOs are very satisfied with their corporate learning function.[6] The most important variable for business success is being managed by the least effective corporate function.

HR is not getting better. From 1995 to 2006, USC's Center for Effective Organizations has monitored changes in the HR profession. Since 1995, each time participants were asked, how much time they spend on strategic activities today versus 5–7 years ago, the participants answered 9 to 10 percent. When the participants were asked how much time they currently spent on these activities, they answered 20 to 23 percent. Each time, participants said they spend twice as much time on strategic activities today than 5–7 years ago—to many, it feels like their job has changed, but it hasn't. According to the data, they spent 21.9 percent of their time on strategic activities in 1995 and 23.5 percent in 2004—no significant change. The profession has talked about being strategic, trained for it, and outsourced administration to make room for more strategic work., but there has been very little change in the time spent on strategic activities or the perceived business added value of the function. What's going on?

For decades, HR has claimed to be on a path to a more value-added function and has asked business leaders for time as it builds new capabilities. There is little convincing data to indicate that the profession's current path is delivering more business value than in the past, and more time will not solve the problem.

Many line executives place the blame on a lack of accountability or substandard people. I disagree on both accounts. Neither more accountability nor different people will fix the problem. The problem is HR's model—the structure, shared values, systems, and skills. Sure, HR programs are better, administration is being outsourced, and e-learning is replacing classroom learning. But these are all parts that fit the old engine. Today's model has never changed, and it continues to produce precisely what it was originally designed to produce—good policies, programs, administration—but that's not what today's business leaders need. The solution is a new approach—a new Human Capital Strategy (HCS)—that delivers performance improvements that produce a sustained competitive advantage.

## Shifting to a New Approach

The modern HR model was created in the 1960s for a personnel department that was responsible for people-related administrative duties and employee relations. It was, and is, based on the premise that the personnel department takes care of administration and employee relations issues so that managers can focus on business results. Today's model has several barriers that prevent it from adding measurable value for customers and shareholders. (They are summarized in Table I-1.)

*Table I-1. A comparison of today's HR model with the Human Capital Strategy.*

| TODAY'S HR MODEL | HUMAN CAPITAL STRATEGY |
| --- | --- |
| Unclear aim | Clearly defined strategy |
| Unclear accountabilities | Clear capabilities and accountabilities |
| Egalitarian | Focus on critical roles |
| Ad hoc and disconnected | Comprehensive and integrated |
| Undisciplined and unmanaged | Measured and managed like financial capital |
| Focused on internal customers | Focused on external customers |
| Program-centric | Results-oriented |
| Reactive | Proactive and focused on year-over-year improvements |

- *Today's model does not have a clear aim.* It does not define how human capital contributes to business results. C. K. Phahalad of the University of Michigan Business School has often chastised HR for its lack of theory or defined position on how it adds value. Does your organization have an end-state blueprint (i.e., what success looks like) or a strategy for systematically building to that blueprint? *HCS defines how human capital will drive business results and delivers a blueprint of what human capital excellence looks like when it's "done."*

- *Today's model does not define accountability.* It is not clear who is accountable for human capital excellence—line managers or HR. Within HR, which unit is accountable for year-over-year improvements in leadership capabilities—staffing, training, compensation, or talent management? Nobody is in charge, and with no one in charge, progress is not possible. *HCS defines the organizational capabilities and accountabilities required to deliver the human capital strategy.*

- *Today's model is egalitarian.* It confuses the important value of all people being of equal worth with the idea that all roles are of equal worth. In fact, all roles are not equally important to customers and shareholders: Some provide significantly more value than others. Focusing investments in roles that are most important to customers and shareholders yields greater returns. In a Hollywood movie, the leading actors are more important to the success of the film than members of the lighting team. That is not to say that lighting is unimportant to the film or that the lighting professionals are not first-class people. They just are not as important to the experience of the moviegoer as the lead actors. *HCS provides a system for improving performance of those in critical roles.*

• *Today's model is ad hoc and disconnected.* It begins with disconnected best practices and world-class programs. Managers continually receive new programs and instructions, but in service to what end-state? Growing human capital requires a top-down approach that begins with a clearly defined theory and a blueprint of success. The system must be built and sustained to deliver component parts for the blueprint that are comprehensive and integrated. As previously mentioned, an automobile engine needs interoperable parts to operate, and having most of the parts will not deliver most of the performance. It might deliver none. *HCS programs are sufficiently comprehensive and integrated to deliver the Human Capital Strategy.*

• *Today's model is undisciplined and unmanaged.* It has no ability to measure changes in human capital or to make progressively better decisions about people and organizations. It reliably measures activities such as average days of training per employee, the percent who received a written appraisal, and bonus differentiation between top and bottom performers. What it doesn't ask is the critical question of whether human capital capabilities and performance are improving over time. *HCS measures and manages human capital with the same discipline that one measures and manages financial capital.*

• *Today's model is internally focused.* It views HR as a supplier and line managers as customers rather than as business partners. HR delivers to the internal customer, even if that is the wrong thing from the perspective of the external customer. *HCS views the external customer as the customer whereas HR administrative activities have an internal customer.*

• *Today's model is focused on programs rather than results.* It defines success as world-class programs rather than world-class people. Look at job ads for talent management roles on any Internet job board or talk to executive search consultants. Companies are searching for professionals who have experience with world-class leadership programs. They are not looking for a track record of building world-class leaders. *HCS views programs as a means, not an end.*

• *Today's model is reactive.* It treats people issues the way a physician treats incoming patients: by reacting to problems and by addressing symptoms. Today's unfulfilled ideal is HR plans that fully align to annual business plans. However, in addition to reacting to annual business challenges, companies must create the business analogue to a wellness program—a systematic and disciplined approach for year-over-year human capital growth. *HCS is a systematic approach to year-over-year capability and performance improvements.*

## Why This Book Was Written

Executives often say that people are the only real source of competitive advantage, but few can clearly explain what that means. If people truly are a company's most important asset, shouldn't executives know whether their assets are more or less valuable each year? Few companies know this; in fact, they don't even know what "more valuable" means or how to measure it. These same companies have very sophisticated models for predicting product performance or customer choices. Think of the potential performance improvements if companies used those same analytics for predicting the impact on business performance of decisions around human capital. And what if it was possible for companies to systematically learn through experience to make progressively better human capital decisions each year?

I believe that in most companies, sustained competitive advantage comes from a more productive workforce—better solution sellers, call center reps, store managers, and/or product development engineers. Get the people and organization equation right, and the organization will win. However, after twenty years in HR, I have seen almost no examples of a defined end-state blueprint for success or systems that reliably deliver measurable human capital improvements. The finger of blame points in many directions. Where is the general manager, and why does he/she not insist on managing human capital as a business asset? Where is HR, and why won't the department accept accountability for results that matter to customers and shareholders? HR is locked into a paradigm where subprofession excellence, world-class programs, and a "seat at the table" are the ultimate measures of success. Until HR breaks out of this paradigm, it will continue its decades-long tradition of speeches and articles about potential value, but never realize it.

Companies will know they have arrived when they can answer two questions:

1. Is your human capital more valuable than your competitors' human capital?

2. Has your human capital improved year-over-year?

This book will enable both general managers and HR professionals to create a blueprint of human capital success and a strategy and system for achieving it. In so doing, we must "blow up" today's HR paradigm and question many of its assumptions.

The bottom line is that when it comes to systematically improving our most valuable asset, the model is wrong. Why else would decades of speeches, articles, and training on strategic HR have failed to move the needle? We have often heard that "Insanity is continuing to do the same thing and expecting a different result." How many more changes will you make in your appraisal program, incentive schemes, management development courses, and HR partnering workshops before you admit that they don't really work? It's not the programs—it's the model.

Let's blow up today's model and replace it with a fundamentally new Human Capital Strategy.

## Notes

1. G. Hamel, "The What, Why, and How of Management Innovation," *Harvard Business Review* (February 2006).

2. E. Lawler, J. Boudreau, and S. Mohrmon, *Achieving Strategic Excellence: An Assessment of Human Resource Organizations* (Stanford, Calif.: Stanford Business Books, 2006), pp. 21–22.

3. C. K. Phalalad and G. Hamel, "The Core Competence of the Corporation" (HBR OnPoint Enhanced Edition), *Harvard Business Review* (March 31, 2007).

4. *CEO Briefing: Corporate Priorities for 2006 and Beyond*, Economist Intelligence Unit, 2006.

5. Accenture, *Accenture High Performance Workforce Study*, p. 64. Figure II-17 (2006). http://www.accenture.com/NR/rdonlyres/D55AA2A6-850F-4589-AADB-553C10A71 09D/0/Accenture_High_Performance_Workforce_Study_2006_v2.pdf.

6. Ibid., p. 71. Figure II-28.

*Part One*

# DESIGNING

## THE

## BLUEPRINT

# Chapter One

# A New Source of
# Competitive Advantage

*"If you don't have a competitive advantage, don't compete."*

—JACK WELCH

As the world's economy globalizes and competitors proliferate, competitive advantage—a compelling reason to do business with an organization—has become increasingly important. In his 2005 book *The World Is Flat*, columnist Thomas Friedman discusses how technology and the Internet are "leveling the playing field" for business. Friedman reports that today, professionals in underdeveloped countries such as India, China, and the nations of Eastern Europe are increasingly able to compete in developed countries for business opportunities once considered local.

A few years ago, designing a company logo was a task assigned to the local printing shop. Not anymore. I recently redesigned my business logo. Instead of going to a local shop, I contracted on the Internet with a company that, for a low price, sent my request for a proposal to logo designers across the world. I received six sample designs, chose the best one, e-mailed my recommended changes, and ended up a happy customer. How can the local printer compete with thousands of highly educated designers across the world? It's pretty difficult. No business wants to acquire new customers by bidding against a host of competitors across the globe, but that is our world today. How can a company stand out from the pack? Is competitive advantage truly possible?

## Maintaining Competitive Advantage

It may be difficult, but maintaining competitive advantage is a requirement, not an option. No business can survive if customers do not have a compelling reason to buy its goods and services. It is difficult to imagine anything more important to the success of an organization. Yet how many companies in numerous industries—television, telecommunications, computer hardware, banking, retail—have a sustained competitive advantage? Creating a source of competitive advantage has become a real challenge.

Perhaps the most common approach to creating competitive advantage is to be less expensive than competitors. For industries that are truly commoditized and hence actively competing for customers, cost seems to be a logical option. However, competing on cost is a difficult game to win. In addition, competition comes not only from small players in underdeveloped countries but from large corporations in developed countries. Europe's Accor Motel 6 chain welcomes a commoditized business environment. So too do Southwest Airlines, Wal-Mart, and the retail chain Carrefour. The aggressive cost structures of these companies have made them profitable with what Wal-Mart calls "Everyday Low Prices."

An alternative to the everyday low price model is to compete on cost through promotions. This strategy attempts to create micro-periods of competitive cost advantage. However, improving profits through promotions is also becoming increasingly difficult. For years, airlines have been able to match competitor promotions within days. Today, however, this may not be enough. Companies like Dell have shown that they can successfully counter a competitor's marketing campaign within twenty-four hours. Back when competitive responses were slower, a surprise promotion could ensure a company of several weeks of increased sales volume, albeit at lower margins. When competitors quickly match a promotion, the expected sales spike may last only a few days. For the weeks thereafter, sales volume returns to normal, but at a lower margin.

The next most common method of creating competitive advantage is through innovative products and services. However, today, in many industries, matching a new offer does not take long. In financial services, for example, new offers and services are frequently countered in a matter of weeks or less. Think about consumer electronics. As a consumer, which company do you think consistently produces the best products? Even in the high technology industry, product innovation may not be sufficient to maintain competitive advantage. During the 2006 supercomputer wars between IBM, NEC, and Cray, the supercomputer champion seemed to change monthly. In the summer of 2006, Apple tied together a cluster of Macs to create the world's third fastest supercomputer. Hard to believe, but even supercomputing seems to be commoditized.

The point is that traditional sources of competitive advantage such as cost and product are becoming more and more difficult to maintain. If survival depends on maintaining a compelling reason for customers to choose one business over another—and it does—the playing field is tougher today than yesterday and will become even more difficult tomorrow as competitors and technologies proliferate.

What, then, is the formula for creating sustained competitive advantage? That was precisely the purpose of the book *Good to Great* by Jim Collins (HarperCollins, 2001). The *Good to Great* research team set out to determine why some companies have been able to sustain success over a long period of time. The book profiled a number of successful companies in highly commoditized industries,

*Figure 1-1. Which company consistently produces superior products?*

were profiled in the book, including Philip Morris, and Nucor Steel. Also included were Krogers, Walgreens, and Circuit City—all competitors in the demanding retail sector and all companies with large numbers of competitors that sell many identical products. Sustained competitive advantage is possible, even in the most commoditized industries.

How did these companies do it? They did it through excellence in people and organizational capabilities. They did it through human capital. Great companies continually improve the health of the goose, rather than exclusively focusing on the golden eggs. Specifically, these companies found the right leader (what Jim Collins calls "Level 5 Leadership"), who put together a great executive team (what Collins calls the "Right People on the Bus"). The new executive team defined a source of competitive advantage (Collins's "Hedgehog" concept) through a documented vision and strategy, and they created and executed a systematic, highly disciplined process for building the specific capabilities needed to deliver the vision and strategy (Collins's "Flywheel"). *Good to Great* told us *what* was important for creating sustained competitive advantage. The book you are reading now provides instruction on *why* it is important and *how* to create a roadmap to achieve that end.

## Competing on Human Capital: What's It Worth?

What is effective Human Capital Management worth to the bottom line? It's hard to say because so few companies have systematic plans for growing human capital. For those with such plans, few can state with confidence whether their human capital is improving year-over-year. Since we do not know precisely what competing on human capital is worth, let's begin with what we do know.

• *We know human capital accounts for a significant portion of operating costs.* Several decades ago, analysts forecasted a shift to a service economy. The service economy grew as expected; in fact, in many advanced economies, more than 75 percent of GDP is now produced by services.[1] In the United States, GDP from services grew from less than half of the economy in the 1950s to 70 percent today.[2] As the service economy grew, so did labor costs. In fact, labor costs are now the single largest component of U.S. business expenses at approximately 44 percent of GDP. Effectively managing such a large expense has potential value.

 • *We know that the intangible value of the world's top 150 corporations (by market capitalization) rose from $800 billion in 1985 to $7.5 trillion in 2005.*[3] The *McKinsey Quarterly* cited a new human capital performance metric—profit per employee—as a much more powerful lever for predicting market capitalization growth than the traditional Return on Invested Capital (ROIC) measure. Want better market capitalization? Improve profit per employee. Want better profit per employee? Build a Human Capital Strategy and measure and manage it with discipline.

 • *We know that in people-intensive businesses, small improvements in employee productivity translate into big financial returns.* The Boston Consulting Group reports that returns in people-intensive businesses (e.g., law firms, consultancies) are particularly sensitive to small changes in operations performance because they require fewer assets than traditional businesses.[4] The authors of the report explained that a 5 percent improvement in employee productivity increases profits by 15 percent of assets (because employee costs are approximately three times the value of assets) and increases economic profit by 50 percent (because economic profit is typically 10 percent of employee costs). Bottom line: Every 1 percent increase in productivity improves profits by 10 percent. A little change in human capital productivity creates a big impact in the bottom line.

 • *We know that market analysts are looking more and more to human capital as they assign market value to companies.* As Ahmed Bounfour (2003) writes:

> It is now largely recognized that balance sheets provide less and less a fair picture of a company's value. This is particularly true of high-tech established companies . . . but more importantly, especially in a very service-oriented economy the physical paradigm is no longer adopted to the measurement of corporate assets.[5]

*Table 1-1. Analysts' ten most important nonfinancial variables.*

| VARIABLE | RANK |
|---|---|
| Execution of corporate strategy | 1 |
| Management credibility | 2 |
| Quality of corporate strategy | 3 |
| Innovation | 4 |
| Ability to attract and retain talented people | 5 |
| Market share | 6 |
| Management expertise | 7 |
| Alignment of compensation with shareholders' interests | 8 |
| Research leadership | 9 |
| Quality of major business processes | 10 |

Which nonfinancial variables provide a good picture of value? Table 1-1 presents the top ten nonfinancial variables considered by analysts,[6] most of which are covered in this book.

- *We know that Fortune's Most Admired Companies are better at managing human capital than their peers.* A 2005 Hay Group study found that *Fortune*'s Most Admired Companies had distinctive approaches for:

  - Attraction and retention of talent
  - Organizational culture
  - Leadership development
  - Performance management
  - Strategy implementation
  - Responding to economic uncertainty
  - Success in execution
  - Fostering innovation[7]

The story is consistent: The differentiating variable for sustained business performance is effective management of human capital. So, how are companies doing in systematically improving this potential source of competitive advantage? Not so well.

## The Need for a New Paradigm

When it comes to improving business performance through people, maybe the correct question is not "How are we doing?" but "Where are we going?" What is the end-state vision, the blueprint of human capital success? In a recent *Yahoo! Finance* column, Ram Charan mentioned that boards are now adding "employee satisfaction" to CEO performance objectives.[8] Is that the right measure for assessing the health of a company's human capital, or was employee satisfaction chosen because boards do not know what else to measure? Most analysts, board members, and CEOs believe that human capital is critically important. They just don't know what human capital is.

Today's approach to managing human capital looks suspiciously like the 1950s model for managing manufacturing. After World War II, manufacturing was the world's economic engine. The success or failure of industrial companies was largely contingent on improving manufacturing efficiencies and product quality. At that time, there were few systematized approaches for improving manufacturing capabilities.

In 1950, W. Edwards Deming introduced a new paradigm—a blueprint—called statistical process control (SPC), which fundamentally changed manufacturing in Japan and eventually across the world. Deming's work was influential in changing the world's perception of Japanese-manufactured products, so that "Made in Japan" was no longer viewed as a sign of low quality but one of the highest quality. SPC is essentially a system that breaks down manufacturing processes into component parts and continually improves system output by measuring and managing performance of each part. If all the parts work, the system produces the expected results.

Is it possible to build an SPC-like system where measuring and managing human capital with discipline produces similarly dramatic performance improvements? It is. The time is right to do for human capital what Deming did for manufacturing—to build a blueprint of success and replace the current HR model with a disciplined and measured Human Capital Strategy that delivers annual improvements in critical organizational capabilities.

## Human Capital Management

What is the difference between human resources management and Human Capital Management (HCM)? Human resources management—which we will refer to simply as HR hereafter—represents all of the people-related activities in an organization. This includes employee records, payroll, benefit design and administration, labor relations, labor law, government relations, and so on. HCM is a subset of HR. It is system for enabling the business to meet its short-term and long-term business objectives by improving the performance of those in critical roles. Administrative and employee relations are subordinate to HCM, and their activities must align to the chosen system. For example, HR would need to determine which benefits were necessary to recruit and retain best-in-industry talent in critical roles, and how the company's relationship with unions would support the Human Capital Strategy.

HCM is founded upon a human capital theory—a statement of how human capital contributes to business success. It is critically important to understand the theory you currently use at your company and then choose the theory you will embrace going forward. There is certainly a theory in place at your organization today that is driving a multitude of daily decisions. You may not know what that theory is, but it is there, and it is impacting the way you work. Let's look at a few theories in use today:

- *Theory 1:* Employees need to be protected from the company. HR protects employees.
- *Theory 2:* Happy people are more productive. HR makes sure employees are happy.
- *Theory 3:* Employee lawsuits hurt the bottom line and the brand. HR reduces lawsuits.
- *Theory 4:* Line managers need to focus on making money. HR must remove people issues to enable line managers to focus.

Think about how an approach to a given business issue varies depending on the accepted theory. Those who accept Theory 1 tend to screen decisions to a standard of fairness and equity, with a core task of policy development and enforcement. A core task for those who accept Theory 2 may be company parties, clubs, and birthday greetings. To Theory 2 folks, great leadership may be measured by leadership style rather than by business results. Bottom line: The response to business problems varies widely depending on the underlying theory in place. Explicitly defining your current and desired human capital theory is the important first step in Human Capital Strategy.

The theory of HCM is simple: When people in critical roles outperform their competitor peers, a company gains competitive advantage. HCM is a system for improving the performance of those in critical roles. The operating principles that underlie the HCM theory were presented in the Introduction, but let's briefly look at them again. (You may wish to refer to Table I-1 in the Introduction.)

## The Critical HCM Components

Outperforming competitor organizations in areas of corporate core competencies requires performance excellence in three critical roles:

1. Effective executive teams
2. Leaders who deliver results
3. Key position excellence

In addition, Human Capital Management includes a fourth factor, an organization-wide enabler called workforce performance, which includes such factors as strategic alignment, culture, appraisal, and pay. Think of the critical roles as seeds and workforce performance as the soil. These four components constitute the Human Capital Strategy. If performance on each strategic component is excellent, the organization will have sustained competitive advantage through people. Chapters 4 through 7 provide in-depth examinations and methods for improving performance on each strategic component. Here is a quick preview of each.

HCS Component 1: Effective Executive Teams. *Are your executive teams better this year than last year?* What does "better" mean? Notice the difference between these questions and today's approach to executive teaming. Today's approach is program-centric and bottoms-up. Consulting firms advise executive teams to address team decision making, participate in a trust-building programs, etc. The HCM approach is top-down. It begins by defining executive team performance—the three to five most important outputs for the executive team—and then builds a system for improving performance on each output.

How can you know if an executive team is "better" than it was last year? Use a scorecard like the example is presented in Table 1-2. In an actual case, executive team members would set their own team

*Table 1-2. A scorecard for assessing executive team performance.*

| EXECUTIVE TEAM RESULT | PHASE 1 | PHASE 2 | PHASE 3 |
|---|---|---|---|
| Strategy | Formalized strategy development process | Strategy development includes a variety of stakeholders | Strategic goal alignment from top to bottom |
| | Broadly communicated strategies | All managers can state the strategic objectives and critical success factors | Ongoing market sensing and feedback |
| Execution | Makes costs budget | Meets key customer, operational, and financial objectives most of the time | Reliably meets customer, operational, and financial quarterly objectives |
| | Business unit productivity plans set | All managers know their unit's productivity goal | Productivity improves to plan |
| Culture | Culture operationalized and accepted by employees | Systematic, measured approach for culture improvement set | Score improvements to plan on defined cultural dimensions |
| Structure | Plan to reduce unnecessary bureaucracy | Unrelenting fight against bureaucracy seen as a cultural hallmark | Employees feel unnecessary bureaucracy is under control |

results and definitions of success from Phase 1 through Phase 3. An annual or biannual team discussion will enable the team to assess its year-over-year progress. In addition, such discussions ensure that all team members define executive team outputs in the same way. In so doing, the scorecard simplifies their role. Whether the company's executive teams are improving or not will no longer be unknown.

**HCS Component 2: Leaders Who Deliver Results.** *Are your leaders better this year than last year?* Think of the financial investments that go into building leaders. Then consider that few can answer this most basic question, The reason is that few companies have defined "better." We spend vast amounts of time and money to improve "it"—we just don't know what "it" is.

*The only true measure of leadership is sustained business results.* These results must be achieved in a way that strengthens the company's values and culture. Leadership styles, personalities, and skills used to deliver business results may be very different; isn't that what diversity is really all about? Unfortunately, in companies with leading HR systems today, programs do not consistently deliver results that matter to shareholders, customers, or employees. Leadership competencies seem to be overtaking business results as the critical determinant of leadership excellence. Leadership competencies can be quite effective when hiring candidates whose past behavior and performance is unclear and for leadership development (fixing spots that are creating performance problems or helping good leaders become even better). But leadership competencies should not be used to assess leadership performance. The only true measure of leadership performance is sustained business results.

Phil Jackson is a National Basketball Association coach whose teams have won nine NBA titles. The sports media have given Jackson the nickname "Zen Master" because of his unorthodox method of coaching players "holistically." Is Jackson a successful leader? It depends on how one defines success. If success is assessed by results, the answer is an emphatic "yes." If success is assessed by a leadership competency model, the answer might be "no." Jackson does not lead like a typical basketball coach.

The problem with our definition of "sustained business results" is that it is too high-level to be useful. So, let's make it useful. The first step is to objectively define "business results." That shouldn't be too difficult: Profit, revenue, and customer satisfaction quickly come to mind. These performance results become lagging indicators (factors that follow other events). The next step is to define leadership results—the three to five things the leader must deliver to achieve sustained performance results. *Improving performance on a set of leadership results that are most predictive of business results is the key to growing leaders.*

In many cases, leadership results vary by leadership position and level. Leadership results for unit retail managers are different from leadership results for the head of manufacturing. At a high enough level of abstraction, it is possible to create one-size-fits-all leadership results; that is the assumption behind corporate leadership competencies. However, this approach is unlikely to provide the performance lift of a more focused model.

Think about the methods that marketing professionals use to maximize revenue. In marketing, it is possible to create a one-size-fits-all customer value proposition and one-size-fits-all marketing programs, but most marketers choose to segment the market and focus on selling to customers segment by segment. Similarly, it is possible to create a generic model of leadership through a corporate leadership competency model, but would you expect that to be as effective as a segmented model? As with marketing, the trick is to balance the costs (i.e., complexity) of multiple segments with the benefits. Organizations may choose to segment leaders by organizational level (e.g., supervisor, middle manager, executive), by role (e.g., country manager, retail store manager), or by a combination of both. This is in contrast to global rollouts of corporate leadership programs. Do you have evidence that your organization-wide leadership programs have improved organization-wide leadership?

Table 1-3 presents a partial example of the leadership results required by a country general manager. Notice the difference from a subjectively assessed, competency-based leadership competency model (e.g., drive to achieve, strategic thinking, political savvy).

The results shown in Table 1-3 are different from competencies—they tell country managers what to do to be successful; not whom to

*Table 1-3. Leadership results for a country general manager.*

| LEADERSHIP RESULTS | METRIC | LEVERS | METRIC |
|---|---|---|---|
| Best sales force in the industry | Customer satisfaction with our sales force versus our competitors' sales forces | Right people | Percent at quota within six months of hire |
| | Sales productivity versus competitors | Right skills | Technical test scores |
| | | Right information and tools | Employee survey |
| Integrate global business units and offerings | Percent of total sales as solution sales | Account team organizational design | Role clarity among sales reps |
| | Customer satisfaction withsolutions | | Customer perception of "one sales force" |
| | Average number of products sold with solutions | | Number of joint sales calls |

be. Notice that these results are objectively measured as opposed to subjectively evaluated competencies. (Additional examples are presented in Chapter 5.) As such, there should be few disagreements between boss and subordinate. Contrast this with the inevitable quarrel that begins when the boss says, "Your 'judgment' competency is low."

If a country executive delivers sustained financial results without delivering any of the key leadership results, fine. In the end, success should be defined by lagging indicators. However, if lagging indicators fail to meet defined performance standards, leadership results will help us understand why.

**HCS Component 3: Key Position Excellence.** Key positions are defined here as critical non-management roles that require a higher level of investment than other roles. An example of a key position can be found by looking at IBM. At IBM, big deal makers have no direct reports but can sell multiyear outsourcing deals as large as $1 billion. Fifteen to twenty of the world's best big deal makers can provide all the revenue

IBM needs to grow its business to plan. What's the right pay for a person who can consistently sell billion-dollar deals? Just about whatever he/she wants. Should we care about internal equity with other professions? Nope. This might make many bristle as it seems to violate the value of internal equity, but this decision is consistent with the Human Capital Strategy: Sustained competitive advantage comes through people in critical roles outperforming peers in competitor organizations.

**HCS Component 4: Workforce Performance.** Many executives aspire to run a high-performance organization, but how many can define what that means? Most executives turn to the appraisal and reward systems to drive performance improvements. However, research indicates that the most prominent characteristics of today's best-in-class performance management systems (e.g., forced distributions, multiple appraisals, negative feedback) actually *reduce* productivity. The best productivity drivers (e.g., accurate feedback, emphasis on strengths, opportunity to work on things you do best) are not actively measured or managed yet create performance improvements in excess of 30 percent. We need a blueprint of a high-performance organization and measure and manage to that end. Chapter 7 defines the blueprint as:

1. Strategy and alignment
2. Organizational culture
3. Appraisal and rewards

Defining the main thing to get right is the first step. For the corporation or business units, this might be expressed in terms of a strategy. A core HCM principle is to work top-down: Everything starts from the strategy.

Delivering the blueprint requires that the organization is capable of delivering the strategy. Does it have the right number of people and skills to deliver its commitments? Strategic goals must be carefully cascaded throughout the organization to ensure that everyone is working on issues that are critical to the business and aligned with one another to accomplish the strategy or business plan.

The second step for delivering the blueprint is to ensure that the culture supports the strategy and business plan. The culture defines what gets rewarded . The importance of culture cannot be overstated.

The third step is to create an appraisal and reward system that aligns with the strategy, cascaded goals, and desired culture. There is little evidence that performance appraisals actually improve performance. Do they in your organization? Probably not. That is because performance appraisals are merely parts of a system, and parts, by themselves, cannot deliver business results. How many times has your organization changed its performance appraisal process in the past decade? Does it work yet?

Incentives may need to be considered as well. Are they required, or—as Clayton Christensen of Harvard Business School suggests—are they a substitute for good management where managers pay employees to want what management wants?[9] One wonders if Israel's Mossad (basically, Israel's CIA) uses bonuses to motivate its agents? What about the Green Berets or Navy Seals in the United States? These organization members seem to be quite motivated without endless discussions of incentive plan designs.

In 2003, Michael Beer and Nancy Katz of Harvard Business School investigated executive incentives by surveying 205 executives in thirty countries.[10] They found that the most important reason for creating an incentive plan was to motivate executives to deliver better results. However, the authors state that the executives surveyed "believe that incentives only improve performance slightly, if at all."[11] Executive incentives do make sense if the purpose is to turn fixed costs into variable costs. But if the only way to get top team members to do what's best for the organization is to bribe them, then maybe you have the wrong people on the team. As a parent, I expect my children to do the right thing without payment. In fact, I don't give our dog treats for being obedient, either. Why would it be different when managing executives?

## Executing the Human Capital Strategy

Exactly *what* needs to be done to create sustained competitive advantage may be getting clearer to you. As previously stated, we must improve performance in three critical roles. An execution plan tells us *how* to improve performance improvements on each strategic component. Figure 1-2 presents the processes for building performance improvement plans on each component. The enabler for all three is a high-performance environment.

*Figure 1-2: The performance improvement roadmap.*

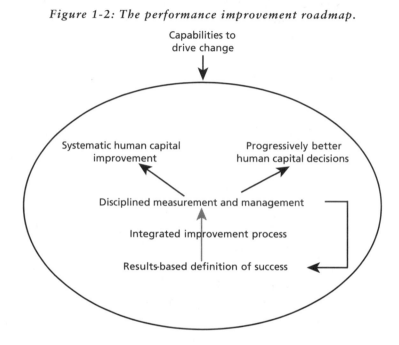

The specific tasks for building each of the strategic components are described in later chapters. You will see that the process and primary tasks are the same for each component. You must have:

- Organizational capabilities sufficient to deliver the strategy
- Results-based definition of success
- Integrated improvement process
- Disciplined measurement and management

## Organizational Capabilities to Deliver the Strategy

The first task for executing any new business strategy is to build organizational capabilities sufficient to deliver the strategy. An American football coach who decides that a passing offense is more efficient than a running offense needs an offensive coordinator experienced in passing, quarterback coaches, a passing quarterback, offensive linemen who specialize in pass blocking, and so on. A strategy without sufficient organizational capabilities gets you nowhere. HCS is no different. If you want systematic human capital growth, you must have an organization and leaders who will drive that growth. However, in today's HR model, no one is accountable for human capital growth. Some may respond that "everyone is accountable"; however, when everyone is accountable, no one is accountable.

Chief Financial Officers (CFOs) do not make all financial decisions, but they are accountable for effectively leveraging their organizations' financial assets. The same should be true of Chief Human Resources Officers (CHROs) and human capital. However, in few cases are CFOs and CHROs held to similar standards.

Chapter 3 presents a detailed analysis of why today's HR model has not, does not, and will not be able to deliver business results. In short, the first reason is that administrative and strategic HR are tangled. Each role supports a different customer (internal versus external), requires different investment models (cost reduction versus ROI), and unique skill sets (policy enforcer versus change agent). Maybe, like sales and marketing, and finance and accounting, it is time to fully separate strategic and administrative HR.

Even for strategic tasks, HR is organized into professional silos (e.g., training, staffing, compensation) that produce world-class parts without a common blueprint (e.g., better leaders, high-performance culture). Profession-aligned silos produce profession-aligned programs. If business results are the objective, the HR organization and systems must be aligned to deliver business results—structure follows strategy. When structure and systems are misaligned with results, it takes very strong and unrelenting leadership to connect the silos in service of a defined business result. When that leadership stops, organization members move back to siloed product development.

This is not to say that the professions do not connect their outputs. They often do, but this usually occurs after products are well underway. It looks like this: "What do you think about this new program?" "It's good. What do you think about ours?" "It's good." Good, but to what end? What are we building and which part did you just complete? Today's bottoms-up approach—starting with a great program and pushing it up and out of the silo—is very different from a top-down approach that begins with the blueprint and defines only the programs and activities absolutely necessary to deliver the desired performance outcomes.

Several transformations must occur to build organizational capabilities sufficient to deliver the HCS. These are introduced below and explained in detail later on.

1. *Align the HR organization around business results.* If the purpose is world-class programs, then today's organization makes sense. But if the purpose is world-class people, then the organization should be aligned to deliver that result. This requires a major structural realignment. One option is presented in Figure 1-3. (This realignment is discussed further in Chapter 3.)

2. *Create top team ownership for human capital growth.* If the top team does not own the results, progress will be difficult. Chapter 3 also presents several effective models for ensuring ongoing line management ownership.

3. *"Brand manage" human capital performance improvements.* Brand management was a management innovation cited by Gary Hamel in his 2006 *Harvard Business Review* article cited in the Introduction of this book.[12] A new paradigm for managing human capital looks a lot like brand management. In this case, the "brands" to

*Figure 1-3. A new organization design for HR.*

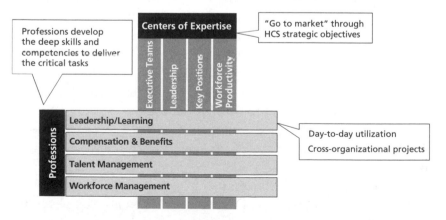

be grown are those in critical roles. For example, if "retail bank manager" is a critical leadership role, then an individual/team creates and leads the execution of a strategy for improving the performance of retail bank managers throughout the world. Success is not good programs; success is a data-based statement that "Our retail branch managers are better this year than last year. This is why the change occurred."

## Results-Based Definition of Success

Once it is clear that the company has the capabilities to execute a business results–based Human Capital Strategy, the organization/team in charge of each of the four components must create a set of metrics that define success. When defining measures of success, I often speak of leading and lagging indicators. (Leading indicators signal future events; lagging indicators follow events.) Each of the four HCS components has one or more lagging indicators that define the desired performance results and three to five leading indicators, which best predict performance on the lagging indicator(s). In other words, if you get these three to five things right, the odds are very good that you will deliver your stated performance outcome.

But what if you get the three to five leading indicators wrong? The answer is that you *will* get it wrong; or at least you will not get it perfect. But that's OK. Has there ever been a new innovation that was perfect right out of the gate? Remember the first generation of Palm Pilots? They were clunky, unreliable tools that only techies could master. If Palm Inc., or its competitors waited until their products were 100 percent right, we might not have electronic organizers today. Over time, your HCS system will capture data to enable your organization to learn from its experience and continually fine-tune its performance indicators.

## Integrated Improvement Process

How many times have you heard, "We tried that, but it didn't work"? There are many reasons why world-class processes and programs don't work. Maybe the program was necessary but not sufficient to solve the problem, or maybe the program was not integrated with other processes and programs. In my experience, the most common reasons for process and program failures are (1) solutions that address symptoms rather than root causes, and (2) focusing on parts rather than addressing the system.

Delivering world-class programs is much easier than producing world-class performance. Business results require finding the root cause and building a system that is sufficiently comprehensive and integrated to deliver a result—which is hard. Business results require a system that is both comprehensive and integrated to solve the root cause.

## Disciplined Measurement and Management

The most common metrics used in HR today measure the efficiency of the HR department: the ratio of HR staff to total employees, the cost of training, the cost per hire, etc. Newer metrics expand on these efficiency measures to include measures of program effectiveness. These new metrics are innovative, but they still are aligned to an internally focused, program-centric model. The metrics focus on program ROI, internal customer satisfaction, or administrative efficiency rather than year-over-year human capital growth.

If we stick to the old HR model, even if we have new measures and more accountability to deliver world-class programs, we are only going to be increasing the production efficiency of things the business may not need. A change in the model, however, may enable us to measure something far more important to the company: the health of its human capital.

# The Outcomes of HCS

## Outcome #1: Systematic Human Capital Improvement

The first outcome expected from a Human Capital Strategy is to know whether or not the system improved performance to plan. This not only answers the question "Did it work?" but also "Where did it work?" Maybe the plan worked in the United States but not in Latin America. Maybe it worked with senior managers but not with supervisors. Capturing data at the lowest level possible, the individual level, helps us answer these questions. It also allows us estimate the value of human capital improvements to the bottom line.

An important role of any executive team is to allocate investment dollars based on an expected return. Gathering and analyzing human capital data provides executive team members with two important data points: (1) to what extent have human capital investments impacted performance, and (2) what are these performance improvements worth to customer satisfaction or to the profit line?

## Outcome #2: Progressively Better Human Capital Decisions

Are leaders across your organization making better human capital decisions this year than they did last year? Is your organization learning through its experience? For example, are competencies or experiences the best predictor for success in the regional manager role? How long does it take, on average, to reach full productivity as a regional manager? What experiences shorten that ramp-up time? All this data probably exists in your organization in separate databases, but someone has to access and analyze it to distill learnings. The real value then is in sharing the learnings with managers across the business to help them make better informed decisions. All this is possible with HCS.

# Conclusion

Profit is generated and sustained when a company provides products and services that meet customers' needs better than competitors do—in other words, when the company has a competitive advantage. Businesses maintain that advantage over time when their core competencies, or the activities that customers value most, are superior to those of their competitors in the eyes of their current and potential customers. The blueprint for creating sustained competitive advantage focuses on improving the performance of those in critical roles, or the roles that are the most important for core capability improvements.

Can a systematic pursuit of human capital growth build sustained competitive advantage? Absolutely. Bill Walsh, one of the great coaches in the history of the National Football League, described his blueprint for building a sports dynasty as a systematic and disciplined process of improving human capital. Walsh stated that his strategy for building a dynasty was first to identify eight positions (quarterback, running backs, linebackers, etc). At the end of the first season, he expected to be the best in the NFL in two positions. At the end of the second season, he would be the best in the NFL in four positions. By year four, he would have a dynasty. Walsh saw sustained competitive advantage as a function of human capital excellence, and he used a time-tested system for producing measurable improvements in human capital. If the team loses Jerry Rice, it needs another Jerry Rice–type receiver to ensure that the system produces the expected output.

If your company followed a similar approach, would it achieve sustained competitive advantage and become an industry dynasty?

# Notes

1. A. Bounfour, *Management of Intangibles: The Organization's Most Valuable Assets* (London: Routledge, 2003).

2. K. Berryman, "The Human Capital Imperative," *McKinsey Quarterly, Special Edition: Organization* (2003).

3. L. Bryan, "The New Metrics of Corporate Performance: Profit per Employee," *McKinsey Quarterly*, Number 1 (2007), pp. 57–65.

4. F. Barber, P. Catchings, Y. Morieux, and R. Strack, *New Rules for People Businesses* (Boston: Boston Consulting Group, 2005).

5. A. Bounfour.

6. J. Low and T. Siesfield, *Measures That Matter* (Boston: Ernst & Young, 1998).

7. "What Makes the Most Admired Companies Great?" *Hay Research Brief* (February 2005).

8. R. Charan, *Yahoo! Finance* (June 26, 2006).

9. C. Christensen, M. Marx, and H. Stevenson, "The Tools for Cooperation and Change," *Harvard Business Review* (2006).

10. M. Beer and N. Katz, "Do Incentives Work? The Perceptions of a Worldwide Sample of Senior Executives," *Human Resource Planning*, Volume 26 (2003).

11. Ibid.

12. G. Hamel, "The What, Why, and How of Management Innovation," *Harvard Business Review* (February 2006).

# The New Human Capital Strategy

*"If you don't know where you're going, any road will get you there."*

—*LEWIS CARROLL,* Alice in Wonderland

In the early 1990s, an American professional football team engaged a consulting firm to help with an executive compensation project. The lead consultant began the discussion by asking, "What is your strategy?" The team owner's reply was, "To win the Super Bowl." "That's a goal," the consultant replied. "What's your strategy? How will your team beat its competitors?" The owner responded, "We don't have anything written, but our coaches and office staff see things similarly." How likely is it that this team will make it to the Super Bowl?

Knowing precisely where one is going and building a plan to get there is the foundation of success in almost any life endeavor. When all team members know precisely what success looks like and align their activities accordingly, progress is almost inevitable. We've all been taught the importance of goals. Goals define end-state success. Goals are the *what*. Strategies are plans for achieving the stated goals. Strategies are the *how*. Goals without clearly defined and aligned strategies are unlikely to be realized.

It seems that when terms like "vision," "mission," and "strategy" are used in general business, they are well understood. However, there is less agreement and understanding about how to improve human capital. Consider the following:

- Should HR have a strategy, or should HR support the business strategy?
- Are today's HR strategies really strategies, or are they annual plans?
- Should an HR strategy include all HR activities, or should it include only the strategic ones?

Despite talk of becoming strategic, the HR profession still struggles to define success. We often hear, "The only true source of sustained competitive advantage is people," but what does that mean? What does it look like when one has arrived, and what path is taken to get there? In speaking about the importance of human capital, Clayton Christensen of Harvard Business School said, "It's time for a common framework and vocabulary around human capital to begin a debate."[1] He's right. The profession is in agreement that it should be "strategic" and add business value, but the profession is less aligned when describing what success looks like or how to get from here to there. Let's start this discussion with a fact-based perspective of the state of HR strategies today.

## The Current State of HR Strategies

Does your company have a strategy for improving the performance of its human capital? Maybe it's inside the overall HR strategy. If so, then we need to see if today's HR strategies are sufficient to improve business performance through people. Take a look at your business strategy and your company's HR strategy and scorecard. Put them next to one another and compare:

- Does the business strategy describe the people and organizational capabilities that are most important for delivering each objective? Are these capabilities reflected in the HR strategy?

- Is the HR strategy a top-down cascade from the business strategy, or is it a project roll-up by HR subprofession (i.e., staffing, compensation, and training)?

- What percent of HR scorecard metrics are directly aligned with the business's strategic objectives? Which metrics matter to external customers?

- How confident are you that your current HR strategy will significantly improve customer and shareholder satisfaction?

Despite decades of books, articles, and conferences advocating a link between business strategies and HR strategies, few companies today are aligned. A 2006 McKinsey survey of executives about challenges to executing business strategy found:

> Executives' concerns about executing and aligning strategy are likely exacerbated by a perceived lack of integration between the company's strategic-planning group and its human resources group. When asked to consider strategic planning's integration with several major corporate functions, respondents rank HR as second-to-last in terms of degree of integration."[2]

It's not just strategic planners who see HR as misaligned. HR leaders are equally critical. As stated in the Introduction, USC's Center for Effective Organizations found that only 9 percent of HR leaders report that they are effective or very effective in connecting HR practices to business performance.

"That may be true for the average organization," you might say, "but that's not the case in blue-chip HR organizations." Don't be so sure. In 2004, a research team from Cornell University's highly regarded Center for Advanced Human Resource Studies (CAHRS) tested that assertion.[3] The team's initial hypothesis was that "surely, almost 20 years and numerous books and articles later, the field of HR has developed a much more tightly integrated structure and is much more highly involved in the development and implementation of business strategy than it was in the 1980s. Or has it?"[3]

The short answer is: "It hasn't." Let's look at the Cornell study. CAHRS is a research partnership with more than sixty large global corporations, with an average employee base of 76,000. These are some of the largest, most successful companies on earth, and these organizations are sufficiently serious about HR excellence to invest in CAHRS. To participate in the study, the CAHRS team invited any of its member organizations that felt they were best practice in HR strategy. Twenty companies agreed. If we make the assumption that all the CAHRS organizations represent some of the world's top HR functions, it would follow that the twenty volunteers might be considered the best of the best in HR strategy. How well do these companies' HR strategies align with their business strategies? Not well. The Cornell team's key findings are presented below:

1. *Bottom-up plans are used.* Rather than using a top-down approach beginning with the business strategy, 75 percent of the participant companies started with HR products and programs and attempted to connect them with business strategies, "standing where they are and reaching out to the business."

2. *Strategies are not owned by line managers.* Only 25 percent of the companies formally involved a line manager in the strategy-setting process, and in more than half the cases, line managers were not asked to approve the strategy. It is unlikely that line managers will assume joint accountability for HR strategies when they are neither involved nor informed of the strategy-setting process.

3. *Strategic components are aligned to HR professions.* Strategic components were typically aligned with HR roles, such as staffing or compensation, rather than with business strategies.

4. *Internally focused activity measures are used to assess performance.* The three most commonly reported metrics were internal customer satisfaction with HR support, ratio of HR headcount to full-time employees, and time to fill open positions.

Put aside for a moment the often-stated professional aspiration of adding business value. Using inductive reasoning, what do these metrics tell you about the *real* HR strategy used in best-of-the-best HR organizations? Is it to drive business performance through people, or is it to improve the efficiency of HR processes? Is the focus on internal or external customer satisfaction? In many cases, if one starts from performance measures and works backward, HR's real strategy is to become a more efficient function.

Why is it that many of the world's best organizations do not align their human capital plans to business strategies? There are two main reasons. The first is that aligning HR strategies to business strategies puts the focus on external customers and results—an approach that is inconsistent with today's internally focused, activity-based HR model. HR is not organized to produce business outcomes; it is organized by HR subprofessions to produce programs to professional standards.

In summarizing the way top companies set HR strategy, the Cornell research team wrote: "Little attention was paid to business outcomes as interviewees responded to [HR strategy] questions. In one sense, this is not surprising because it seems unwise to focus on outcomes over which one has little or no control." The Cornell team is right. HR's structure is driving its strategy. HR is misaligned with the business, and HR executives in many of the world's most respected companies don't see it.

The second reason that business and HR strategies are not aligned is that many line managers delegate people issues to HR and hope for the best. Few line managers have a vision of human capital success.

Think about the way general managers (GMs) manage their unit's finances. Effective GMs do not just delegate day-to-day financial tasks to the finance department. Instead, they stay close to the numbers from quarter-start to quarter-end. They want to know what the numbers are, why they are what they are, and what can be done to push them higher. Compare that with the time GMs spend measuring and managing human capital. Without an end-state picture of human capital excellence, they do not know how to measure, manage, or invest. The result is leadership abdication: Send human capital issues to HR and hope they will figure it out. Most managers have a system for improving financial returns, but few have a system for improving human capital returns.

## Building a Human Capital Blueprint

Before we talk about human capital strategies, let's think about other types of strategies. An effective manufacturing strategy is a written plan for beating competitors on price-quality metrics. A finance strategy might define the three to five most important things to get right for leveraging financial assets to beat competitors and maximize profits. In both manufacturing and finance organizations, there are many activities going on every day, but successful organizations define the most important things to do and align all activities to do them.

The same needs to be true with HR. HR has many administrative and employee relations activities, all of which must support an end-state goal. The problem is that many HR organizations have not defined that end-state goal—what does sustained competitive advantage through people look like? The outcome is HR activities and programs founded on various visions of success, each pulling in a different direction. The remedy is to create a Human Capital Strategy (HCS): a statement of how the organization will use its human assets to beat competitors and maximize profits. HCS components include the human capital theory, vision, and strategic components, as shown in Figure 2-1 and defined in Table 2-1.

Think of human capital strategies as split into two parts, one of which is short-term and the other long-term. The short-term objective is to ensure that people and organizational capabilities are sufficient to

*Table 2-1. The human capital vocabulary.*

| TERM | DEFINITION |
| --- | --- |
| Human Capital Strategy | The plan for how an organization will produce sustained competitive advantage through people. |
| Human Capital Theory | A cause-and-effect description of how people create business value. |
| Human Capital Vision | A blueprint of success; what sustained competitive advantage through people looks like upon completion. Also called the end-state goal. |
| Strategic Components | The most important results for delivering the human capital vision. |

*Figure 2-1. The Human Capital Strategy and its components.*

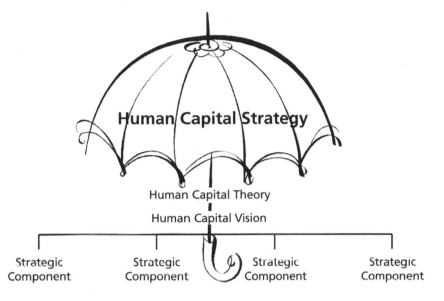

deliver the annual business plan. The long-term objective is to create sustained competitive advantage through people.

The short-term part is technically, not a strategy. It is a human capital plan that supports the business strategy. A strategy is a plan for how to beat competitors. Sports teams have game strategies, marketing organizations have brand strategies, and sales organizations have sales strategies. All of these describe how the organization will beat its competitors. Short-term HR plans that support a business strategy are critically important, but they are not strategies. They are plans. Plans are equally important, but different.

Most discussions of strategic HR focus on plans. Making sure the business can achieve its annual plan *is* the first priority of an HR organization. Examples include mergers or acquisitions, shifting headcount from a low- to a high-growth business, or outsourcing tasks overseas. Success is achieved when line executives and HR leaders agree that they have addressed all the people and organizational issues required to deliver each business objective.

There are many excellent writings on how to align HR activities with business strategies. Some of the best tutorials are *Roadmap to*

*Strategic HR* by Ralph Christensen (Amacom, 2005) and *The HR Scorecard* by Brian E. Becker, Mark A. Huselid, and Dave Ulrich (Harvard Business School Press, 2001). Why haven't the principles in these compelling books been adopted? The problem is the model: Today's HR is misaligned with the task of driving business value. The model rejects great advice and new tools, and more and better programs and methods will not help.

In addition to ensuring the business has the right number and levels of skills to deliver its short-term plans, an effective HCS systematically strengthens the organization's capabilities over time. To illustrate this new paradigm, think of a marketing strategy. Marketing organizations must not only align their marketing calendar to deliver short-term business results. They must also create sustained competitive advantage by strengthening the brand over time. By strengthening the brand, marketing builds a source of sustained competitive advantage. For many years, Coca-Cola has been the world's most powerful brand.[4] People try new Coca-Cola products because they trust the brand. Coca-Cola's brand equity did not happen by chance. It was a result of a relentless and systematic process for growing an important business asset.

Manufacturing is another function with short-term and long-term strategies. Manufacturing functions must produce products to meet short-term business plans. But that is not all; great manufacturers relentlessly and systematically grow their manufacturing capabilities to build sustained competitive advantage over time. Toyota continues to win because it spent years improving its manufacturing capabilities. The company now enjoys sustained competitive advantage through manufacturing excellence.

Jim Collins's *Good to Great* research team found that Coca-Cola and Toyota are not isolated cases. The team learned that companies that are able to sustain success over a long period of time (i.e., they had a sustained competitive advantage) seldom attribute success to any one program or initiative, but rather to a clear vision of how the company will compete and an unrelenting focus on improving the capabilities required to achieve that vision. The research team called this "the Flywheel." It is a metaphor of a large, heavy flywheel that is difficult to turn from a dead stop, but with many unrelenting actions, increases in velocity over time. The Flywheel eventually gains inertia and spins with little help. Both Coca-Cola and Toyota created a vision of how they would compete and the core competencies required to deliver that vision. Both companies created sustained competitive advantage through decades of unrelenting pushes on their Flywheel—brand power at Coca-Cola and manufacturing capabilities at Toyota.

Similar to marketing and manufacturing, improving business performance through people requires effectively setting and executing short-term and long-term strategies. Rather than spending time here discussing how to realign the HR model to fulfill business strategies (the subject of Chapter 3), let's think through a Human Capital Strategy that continually strengthens an organization's competitive advantage over time. Let's build a human capital Flywheel.

## The Human Capital Theory

The first question to answer is: *How does HR create business value?* Several years ago, while involved in a project with a large retail company's HR department, I noticed that the labor law team was the largest corporate HR department. The company employed eight to ten times the number of labor lawyers per employee as its competitors, and four of its six corporate HR executives had been promoted from the legal department. Attorney telephone numbers were on the speed dial of every HR generalist, and daily decisions were routinely screened for legal exposure. HR generalists complained incessantly about the legal team obstructing their work, but the checking and approval process remained intact. What would you say was HR's theory on how it added value to the business?

A second company I supported had been a lead company in a regulated industry for many years. In this company, the focus of HR staff meetings was policy and policy enforcement. Before meetings and on breaks, HR generalists playfully sparred with one another on policy details. ". . . That's right, but she only gets 30 days if she has more than two years of tenure at a company merged before 2001." Peers looked on and cheered as one bested the other. How might you describe the human capital theory at this company?

In the first company, the human capital theory was that lawsuits hurt the bottom line and brand equity. HR added business value by reducing the number of lawsuits. Actual data showed that the total spent in all employee-related legal costs was 1/10,000 of the company's total revenue, a ratio consistent with competitors. Not only did the heavy legal staff not create best-in-class results, it blocked many efforts to improve productivity.

In the second company, the human capital theory was a legacy from a time when the company did not need productivity improvements. Such improvements were seen as creating excessive profits and spurring government-mandated price reductions. The human capital theory was that trouble-free operations were a result of stable processes and relationships. HR added business value in this closed system by improving employee perception of internal fairness and equity. HR executives at both companies talked about business value and strategic HR and truly believed it, but their activities, projects, and decisions were rationally aligned to a deeper, unstated human capital theory. Outside hires who were brought in to add the missing strategic component were quickly rejected as their activities and decisions aligned to a different theory and were viewed as irrational.

What is your organization's human capital theory? Here are a few ways to find out:

- Ask HR executives why they chose a certain decision. Continue asking why over and over until you hit the root.

- Look at the performance objectives of your boss and peers. If you distilled them down to a "main thing," what would it be?

- Look at who gets promoted. What makes them stand out?

- Which are the most powerful HR departments?

- How does the Chief Human Resources Officer spend his/her time? What are the topics of the last ten to twenty all-points CHRO e-mails?

- Ask an HR professional, "What is the most important thing HR needs to get right?"

- Run an activity analysis on HR generalists.

The human capital theory you choose for your company will vary depending on your business circumstance. It is important that you surface and debate the theory as it is and will continue to drive the activities of every HR professional.

## The Human Capital Vision

The important question to answer here is: *What does success look like?* In the mid-1990s, Taco Bell, then a PepsiCo company, was one of the hottest companies on earth. In the middle of its success, John Martin, Taco Bell's CEO, assigned seven of his highest-potential middle managers to a two-year, full-time, multidisciplinary team to reinvent Taco Bell's business model. Martin's vision was "250,000 points of access by the year 2000." He defined a point of access as "wherever someone can buy a Taco Bell product." Taco Bell's new vision was clear, memorable, and measurable.

Given that Taco Bell had about 4,000 stores at the time, 250,000 seemed to be an unrealistic goal. However, the team energetically began work and within a few short months had created a new process that increased store openings from 700 each year to more than 1,200. Martin thanked the team but told them that while that was very good news, the goal was still 250,000 points of access.

The team decided that it needed to think more creatively. At the time, cafeterias were the only place to eat in airports. "What if we put Taco Bells in airports?" the team members wondered. "Let's call them SPODs" (special points of distribution). Soon, Taco Bell SPODs were popping up in airports, stadiums, and strip malls. SPODs quickly added more than 1,000 points of access each year. Again, Martin was grateful but unmoved. The vision was still 250,000.

The team had a few failures—Taco Bell vending machines, frozen burritos—but then they had a brainstorm. Why not use Frito-Lay, another PepsiCo company, to produce and distribute Taco Bell chips and salsa? Within a few months, Taco Bell chips and salsa hit grocery store shelves. Another 50,000 points of access. Good, but still not enough.

The team added another 5,000 points of access through Taco Bell carts, designed to sell products in parks and on street corners. They also created a program for selling burritos to schools for sale in school lunchrooms. This increased store utilization during the morning hours and turned thousands of schools into points of access.

The team missed the 250,000 mark, but they increased points of access from 4,000 stores to well over 100,000 points of access. But innovation isn't free. The effort required a two-year commitment of the highest-potential managers from each function, plus significant consulting fees. The investments were significant; the results were breakthrough.

The Taco Bell story is an example of a clear vision of success that created an explosion of innovation. The story provides three important lessons for setting and executing a human capital vision:

1. An unambiguous statement of success is required.
   - The end-state must be quantifiable and include a measurement of success.
   - The end-state must be time-bound.
   - The statement must be simple and unforgettable.
2. Organizational transformation requires an organizational infrastructure that maximizes the probability of success (e.g., a full-time, dedicated team of the highest-potential performers).
3. Significant and focused investments in time and money are required.

Does your organization have an unambiguous definition of human capital success—what success looks like when you have arrived? If so, is your performance to the vision improving year-over-year?

## Setting the Human Capital Vision

The human capital vision is founded on the human capital theory and attempts to turn the theory into a concrete statement of success. Figure 2-2 presents an example.

Several assumptions lie beneath the vision statement:

- Leading measures are defined by *performance*, not competencies. Competencies are an important means to an end and

*Figure 2-2. A sample human capital vision.*

**Human Capital Vision**

Theory:  When people in critical roles consistently outperform
those in competitor organizations, we win

By [date], we will outperform competitors in the following roles:

- Critical Role 1
- Critical Role 2
- Critical Role 3

---

should be measured and managed as such; but success is industry-best performance, not industry-best people.

- Success is measured against industry benchmarks or primary
competitors. Being world-class is ideal, but it is not required to
deliver business results. Burger King's performance in site selection must be better than McDonald's; it does not need to be
better than Marriott's.

- It is often, but not always, possible to compare performance of
nonmanagement roles to similar roles in competitor companies
(e.g., sales, customer service). It may be more difficult to compare performance of some leaders to their competitor peers.
Can you compare cross-company performance of sales executives or product development leaders? Probably yes, but it might
be more difficult to compare the performance of internal communications managers, retail store managers, or sales managers.

- When performance to competitors cannot be assessed, measure year-over-year changes. Note that performance metrics
will not be perfect. Start with a "B" and improve until you get
an "A." If you wait for an A to begin, you might never do so.

# Strategic Human Capital Components

The human capital vision creates a concrete and measurable definition
of success; the strategic components are plans that describe how to

*Table 2-2. The four human capital strategic components.*

| STRATEGIC COMPONENTS | RATIONALE |
|---|---|
| Effective Executive Teams | Executive teams must continually improve the value they produce for the broader organization. |
| Leaders Who Deliver Results | Leaders must align all activities to achieve the business plan and improve organizational capabilities that enable high performance. |
| Key Position Excellence | Those in nonmanagement positions most important to customers and shareholders must reliably deliver better performance than their peers in competitor organizations. |
| Workforce Performance | The organization must have the structure, systems, and culture to enable great performance. Great performance means higher productivity and better cost structure than competitors'. |

achieve that vision. Achieving the vision requires excellence in four components. (See Table 2-2.) If all four are well-executed, it is likely that your organization will have a sustained competitive advantage through people. The first three strategic components are critical roles—roles that are most important for customer and shareholder satisfaction. The fourth component enables the first three.

## Effective Executive Teams

The key question to ask about the first critical role—effective executive teams—is: *Are our executive teams more effective this year than last year?* The executive teams may include the corporate top team, business unit teams, region/country-level teams, and functional leadership teams. Without a high-performing executive team at the top, little will happen below. Executive teams set the end-state vision and business strategies, and invest time and money to ensure that aspirations turn to business results.

Just as human capital growth requires a top-down, comprehensive, and integrated improvement plan, so do executive teams. (However, that's not the way many internal and external consultants approach executive teaming today.) An effective executive team improvement plan begins when executive team members agree on the team's value-add to the business and define specific activities and measures for realizing that value-add. The work of the executive team is covered in Chapter 4.

## Leaders Who Deliver Results

What is the single most important decision a corporation can make? Arguably, it is choosing the CEO. What about the most important decision for a company's China subsidiary? It's probably choosing the general manager for the subsidiary. At each level, starting from the top and working down, great leaders build the strategy, choose the leadership team, and align the organization.

At McDonald's, except for location, every restaurant is essentially the same—same menu, same prices, same training material, and same store layout. The difference between high-performing and low-performing McDonald's restaurants is almost exclusively a function of the restaurant manager. Take a failing store, import a successful manager, and even with essentially the same crew, the restaurant will recover within thirty days. Great restaurant managers create a culture that delivers the oxymoron of discipline and fun. And when McDonald's restaurant managers are excellent, district and area managers are largely unnecessary. Great managers generally don't need or want HR field support, local marketing support, etc.— they prefer to stand on their own. Not only do great managers grow unit profits, they also reduce system-wide costs. Despite the obvious importance of unit managers at retail organizations, how many companies report year-over-year leadership performance changes of their unit managers?

Twenty-five years of Gallup research concludes that how long employees stay and how productive employees are is determined by their relationship with the immediate supervisor.[5] The world's best recruiting, development, and appraisal processes are useless if managers are not top quality. But what is "top quality," and how do you get from here to there? Chapter 5 discusses aspects of the leadership issue, including how to define top leaders.

## Key Position Excellence

The most important question to answer here is: *Are those in key positions outperforming their peers in competitor organizations?* Too often today, people programs and policies are rolled out system-wide, with programs and policies applying to everyone in the organization.

Making equal investments in all roles seems fair and equitable, but it's bad for the business. Some roles are more important to customers and shareholders than others. The most important roles should be paid well over industry standards, the moderately important ones at or below standards, and the least important ones below standards or outsourced. Training investments should also vary. When we follow the key position approach, we attempt to increase the performance of the 20 percent of positions that produce 80 percent of customer and shareholder value. Think in terms of your own finances: When you allocate your personal investment dollars, do you invest the same amount in every mutual fund, or do your dollar amounts differ by expected return?

The ideal performance measure for excellence in a given position is performance relative to competitors. For sales positions, this may be measured by a customer rating of the sales representative or sales team versus sales reps or teams from competitor organizations. For scientists, it might measure the number of new patents by a scientist or research team that turn into products versus the average of those at competitors. Unfortunately, comparison statistics are not always possible. In these cases, you may choose to use an internal measure of year-over-year performance changes while you continue to search for good comparison measures.

Chapter 6 provides a full discussion of key position performance.

## Workforce Performance

The key question to answer here is: *Has workforce performance improved since last year?* No amount of success in critical role development is possible until the organization has a clear strategy and organizational capabilities aligned to that strategy. The strategic component, workforce performance, is actually the first step in any human capital improvement project. We cannot know which roles are critical until the strategy is set and the organization realigned. We need to have a simple and compelling vision, an aligned organization, a high-performance culture, and an appropriate appraisal and rewards process.

**Simple and Compelling Vision.** The organization must try to answer the following questions:

- Where are we going and why?
- What are the steps for getting from here to there?
- How are we doing and what else needs to be done?

**Aligned Organization.** The second critical success factor is to fully align organizational activities to the strategy and to create a cascade of objectives to ensure that all objectives are delivered. Not only does this focus efforts on the most important tasks; it also exposes tasks that do not directly add business value.

**Performance Culture.** The two statistically most important drivers of a high-performance culture are: (1) fairness and accuracy when providing feedback and assessing performance results, and (2) creating a risk-taking culture.

**Appraisal and Rewards.** The organization must try to answer the following questions:

- Which performance improvement methods have the biggest impact on productivity?
- What is the best way to improve focus, accountability and motivation?

Chapter 7 will help you answer each of these questions.

# Plans That Deliver Business Results

Delivering business results on each strategic component is much more difficult than producing programs for each component. There are several design principles for ensuring that great programs and activities deliver great results for each of the four strategic components. Your plans must be:

- Top-down
- Comprehensive

- Integrated
- Disciplined

## What Is a Top-Down Plan?

The Cornell study discussed earlier in this chapter highlighted the tendency, even in the best companies, to create people-related strategies from the bottom up. This may be similar to plumbers and roofers who begin work without knowing if they are building a house, an office, or a fire station. Often, new projects are generated by a sales manager who learns of a recognition program or by an HR generalist who reads a book and creates a new protocol based on it. When these projects are not aligned to a common blueprint, they may be viewed by line managers as pellets from a shotgun coming toward them. You know you have a problem when managers complain about being awash in new tools, policies, and programs. You may have some great programs, but to what end?

In contrast, top-down–generated plans are crafted to fully deliver a clearly defined end-state measure on each strategic component. A good top-down plan includes just enough tools and programs, but never more than required.

## What Is a Comprehensive Plan?

A comprehensive plan deploys all necessary components to produce the defined business result. When I was a young consultant, a seasoned partner told me, "It's almost never a compensation problem." He was right—the problem is almost never unidimensional.

Seasoned consultants will tell you that most initial client requests are for training or for making appraisal/compensation changes. Employees are seen as either unskilled or unmotivated. In a product-based HR organization, adopting a best-in-class program might be sufficient to declare victory—but it won't necessarily get you the best business results.

A results-based approach is far more challenging. Improving performance requires that incumbents have the right talent, skills, tools, information, job design, performance measures, and so on. If any of those are missing, it may not be possible to deliver a performance result.

## What Is an Integrated Plan?

An integrated plan means that all the parts fit. Improving the performance of people requires that all components of the plan work together. For example, a team-based sales role must use team-based incentives, provide team-based training, and use selection tools that screen for a history of teamwork. If financial incentives are individually based, the team approach is likely to fail, regardless of the quality of the other parts.

## What Is a Disciplined Plan?

A disciplined plan means that accountabilities are clear, deliverables are tightly managed, and progress is known by key stakeholders.* A disciplined plan includes both leading and lagging indicators of success. Lagging indicators represent the final expected result or performance to the end-state vision. Leading indicators are those that are most predictive of lagging indicator success. Delivering results on leading and lagging indicators requires a disciplined approach that pushes the ball forward day after day.

## Comprehensive, Integrated, and Disciplined: An Example

Let's imagine we are putting two groups to work building and executing a plan for improving life satisfaction. The first group uses a bottoms-up approach. One member reads a book on personal finance to help manage money more effectively. Another reads magazine articles on health, and still others may watch a talk show on relationships. How likely is it that the group as a whole will experience a positive shift in life satisfaction?

The second group uses a top-down approach. They begin by creating a clear end-state vision of life satisfaction and a measure of success—a lagging indicator. They agree that a single measure of life satisfaction

---

*A stakeholder is anyone with a critical stake in the outcome. Stakeholders might include directly affected employees, their manager, and the executive team.

is difficult to find, so they create a life satisfaction index from two measures: (1) a perceived happiness rating given by ten friends and family members, and (2) a self-score on a validated survey of satisfaction. The end-state is now operationally defined.

The group's next step is to build a strategy for achieving the end-state. They decide that there are four strategic components for achieving happiness: (1) good health, (2) good friends, (3) a close family, and (4) a job that is fun. Note that these dimensions are results-based rather than activity-based. (See Figure 2-3).

The first component is health. Like life satisfaction, arriving at a single measure for health is difficult, so the team uses a combination of stress test results, days of work lost to illness, and physical strength as a percentage of average strength for gender, height, weight, and age. When there is no "one best" measure, the team collects several measures and triangulates.

Group members realize that the health plan must be comprehensive. They create critical success factors (CSFs) or necessary and (almost) sufficient conditions to achieve success on each CSF. Thus, if a person achieves successful scores on all five health CSFs, he/she will likely be physically healthy. But if, say, all CSFs except blood pres-

*Figure 2-3. A top-down strategy for improving life satisfaction.*

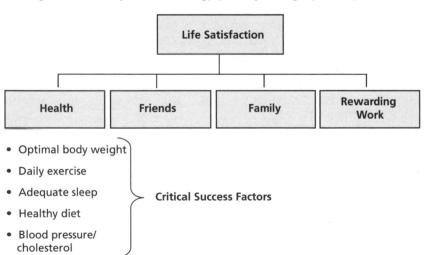

sure/cholesterol are on target, they cannot celebrate because they may be on the road to a heart attack. All parts of their health plan must be integrated with other parts. Finally, their health plan must be disciplined: A great plan that is not executed has no chance of improving satisfaction.

The Human Capital Strategy follows the same approach as this life satisfaction example. We start by defining the end-state blueprint, or the vision. Next, we define the strategic components for achieving that end-state. Then we set the critical success factors to ensure that we achieve each strategic component. Finally, we build a management system for ensuring that we carry out the plan.

# Determining the Optimal Blueprint for Your Organization

The key question to answer here is: *What is the most effective Human Capital Strategy for your organization?* How can you know if your company is improving the performance of its human capital? How can you know if your company is managing its human capital more effectively than its competitors are?

## The Human Capital Lagging Indicator

Is there a single measure that concludes human capital improves year-over-year? Or, should we judge the efficiency of a human capital strategy by measuring changes in each of a set of key positions?

A 2007 *McKinsey Quarterly* article stated that the value of "intangible capital" of the world's top 150 companies, as measured by market value less invested financial capital, increased from $800 billion in 1985 to $7.2 trillion in 2005.[6] However, annual reports still focus on how a company uses its financial capital—not how it is growing its intangible values, the most important of which is human capital.

The McKinsey study examined the thirty largest companies in the world (by market capitalization) over the period 1995 to 2005. They found that the driver of a five-fold increase in profits was a doubling of profits per employee and number of employees. The Return on Invested Capital (ROIC) increased only by one-third during that same period. In other words, human capital measures were a much stronger predictor of market capitalization through profit growth than traditional measures such as ROIC. The world has changed. Effective human capital management, rather than financial capital management, is the most important driver of business value. Here is the equation for predicting profit growth and eventually market capitalization increases:

$$\text{Profit per Employee} \times \text{Number of Employees}$$

You need a high profit per employee and lots of employees. This equation held true for companies like Wal-Mart, with lots of employees and low profit per employee, and for Microsoft, with few employees and high profits per employee. The equation is not perfect, but it's pretty robust and very simple.

Any company can measure its year-over-year change in human capital by applying this formula to answer the question "Are we managing our human capital more effectively than last year?" Companies can also compare the effectiveness of their human capital with those in similar competitor companies. This requires that the companies are identical. Perhaps a better measure is year-over-year performance changes between industry competitors.

## Human Capital Leading Indicators

What if you knew the most important things to do for your organization to grow its profit per employee and market cap? You have a vision and strategy that you can show, statistically, is the best model for *your* organization. This is possible and requires only simple statistics—the stuff you learned in Statistics 101.

Here is how it works. We've made an assumption that four strategic components are both necessary and sufficient for delivering the human capital vision. Thus, if an organization scores well on all four, it will have a sustained competitive advantage. However, whether these four truly matter to your organization's business results is still an educated guess. Let's turn gut level feelings into facts.

Building the optimal Human Capital Strategy for your organization requires systematically tracking performance over time and isolating re-

*Figure 2-4. Identifying relative impact by strategic
component on the human capital vision.*

lationships between lagging indicators (e.g., revenue growth, profit, customer satisfaction) and leading indicators (i.e., the four strategic components). This requires a basic regression equation between each of the four strategic objectives and one or more lagging indicators. The result will tell you the relative impact on profit per employee of each of the four strategic components. (See Figure 2-4.)

Scores for each of the four strategic components are regressed on profit per employee. Remember, this is illustrative—it's not real data. If this were real data, key position excellence would be the strongest driver of operating profits because it has the biggest correlation coefficient ($r = .56$), followed by effective executive teams ($r = .44$) and workforce performance ($r = .42$). The bigger the correlation coefficient ($r$), the more impact the strategic component has on profit. In this example, key position excellence has eight times more impact on profit than leaders who deliver results (i.e., .56 is eight times more than .07). If we want changes in profit per employee, we would be wise to make bigger investments in key position excellence than in leadership development. (Again, remember that this is not real data.)

If this data appeared in your organization, you might conclude that leadership performance ($r = .07$) is not related to profits. This might be because in your organization, leadership really isn't that important. Alternatively, it might indicate that you chose the wrong leadership roles or the wrong leadership results, or that the results were inaccurately measured. Any of these hypotheses can be easily tested if you have the kind of data recommended throughout this book. (There is more on how to measure leadership in Chapter 5.)

You might wonder, "What if there are other important strategic components we should have measured but didn't?" Let's say the top team chooses these four components to begin, but they also feel that "across-the-board skills" might be a good predictor—they're just not sure. The team might choose to add the new measure "skills" to the model as a test component and analyze it behind the scenes. Let's say that regressing "across-the-board skills" produces a coefficient of .62. That would mean that compared to the other four components, improving across-the-board skill levels was the most important thing to get right to improve profits. The team may then choose to eliminate leadership as a strategic component and add across-the-board skills. (See Figure 2-5.)

By capturing and analyzing data over time, your organization can estimate the financial impact of performance changes on each of the strategic components and make better informed investment decisions. Remember that $y = ax + b$ equation from Statistics 101 that you swore you would never use? You need it now. Plug in $x$ as the leading indicator and out pops $y$ as the estimated value of the lagging indicator. "If we improve key position performance by $x$ percent, we will increase profits by $y$ percent." It's really no different from using retirement calculators where changing the leading indicators (e.g., years to retirement, money saved per year, percent annual investment increases) changes the number of work years left—the lagging indicator. Any graduate student in statistics can do this work for you.

*Figure 2-5. Updating the relative impact by strategic component on the human capital vision.*

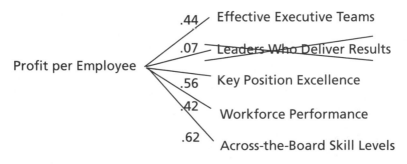

# Conclusion

Systematically improving human capital has been an unfulfilled dream for the past thirty years. The primary reason is that few line managers or HR professionals have defined an end-state vision of success. There is no lack of activity, but without a clearly defined end-state, line managers, heads of Centers of Excellence, and HR business partners are all rowing in different directions.

The first question to answer focuses on the HR department. It asks: "What is HR's role in creating business value?" This will impact every activity and decision of HR professionals. What is the theory of HR today, and what will it need to be in the future?

The second task is to define what sustained competitive advantage through people looks like for your organization. It answers the question: "What does it look like when it's done?" The human capital vision is the blueprint or end-state vision of success.

The third task is to determine the three to five most important things to deliver the human capital vision—the strategic components. We have discussed four generic strategic components: effective executive teams, leaders who deliver results, key position excellence, and workforce performance. If a company exceeds the performance of competitors on all four, it will have a sustained competitive advantage.

The fourth task is to determine whether the four strategic components are the best fit for your organization. This requires putting a stake in the ground on the most important components and measuring them over time to determine whether they are truly the most important things for driving your business results.

# Notes

1. Personal conversation with Clayton Christensen, April 17, 2007.
2. "Improving Strategic Planning: A McKinsey Survey," *McKinsey Quarterly*, Web Exclusive (September 2006).
3. P. Jacobsen, S. Snell, and P. Wright, "Current Approaches to HR Strategies: Inside-Out versus Outside-In," *Human Resource Planning*, 27 (4) (2004), p. 36.

4. http://images.businessweek.com/ss/06/07/top_brands/source/1.htm.

5. M. Buckingham and C. Coffman, *First, Break All the Rules* (New York: Simon & Schuster, 1999), pp. 11–12.

6. L. Bryan, "The New Metrics of Corporate Performance: Profit per Employee," *McKinsey Quarterly*, Number 1 (2007), p. 57.

# Creating Capabilities to Execute the Blueprint

*"Many innovations fail . . . because the responsibility to build these businesses is given to organizational units that aren't capable of succeeding . . . the very capabilities that propel an organization to succeed in sustaining circumstances will systematically bungle the best ideas for disruptive growth. An organization's capabilities become its disabilities when disruption is afoot."*

—*CLAYTON CHRISTENSEN AND STEPHEN KAUFMAN*[1]

S everal years back, I witnessed a heated conversation between a newly appointed GM who was the head of U.S. retail operations and his vice president of HR:

> GENERAL MANAGER: "We hire hundreds of thousands of new employees every year, yet we use no selection process or tools. We need a good selection system."

HR VP: "We designed a good selection system last year, but your organization didn't use it."

GENERAL MANAGER: "Then . . . it must not have worked."

HR VP: "Oh, it worked. It worked very well! You guys said you wanted it, we delivered it, and you didn't use it."

The HR VP was internally focused and program-based. His customer was the general manager and that customer wanted a selection tool. His HR organization needed to build a tool to his customer's specifications. Whether it was needed or not, or whether it worked or not, was not his problem; he, and the rest of HR were accountable for developing state-of-the-art programs and tools, not for business results. The GM saw the situation differently. He saw his HR VP as accountable for solving a business problem. Throwing a "world-class" tool over the fence was not what the GM was expecting.

This conversation highlights a critical question: "Who is accountable for year-over-year human capital growth?" In today's model, the answer is not clear. Line managers point to HR, and HR points back to the line. HR sees itself as accountable for delivering programs to internal customers and for being advisers. In the Human Capital Management model, HR's role is *not* to be a business adviser but to be the corporate leader for ensuring year-over-year human capital growth. I have interviewed many candidates for senior HR positions who describe their accomplishments as sitting in the right meetings (being at the table) and giving great advice. My response is always: "But what have you accomplished that has created value for customers or shareholders?" Most interviewees see that as a very odd question, and few can answer it.

Certainly, HR cannot be solely accountable for human capital growth; human capital is a shared accountability. If HR and line management are not equally accountable, little will change. HR's role is to accept accountability for creating business value through people and then provide leadership for ensuring that line managers are equally accountable. HR professionals must stop blaming line management for not buying in and consider lack of line manager buy-in as an HR failure.

As you read this chapter, you will see that today's roles and accountabilities of HR and line management are often unclear. You will understand why we are in this leadership vacuum and what you and your company can do to fix it.

## Today's Human Resources Function

Throughout history, virtually all breakthroughs required replacing a current model with a fundamentally different paradigm. Scientific examples include germ theory and the theory of relativity. Federal Express and Amazon.com are business examples of a paradigm shift, and W. Edwards Deming's statistical process control is an example of a professional shift. In each case, these new paradigms emerged and completely challenged existing "truths." The HR profession has yet to go through its paradigm change.

Think of today's HR model as an engine with four elements: (1) structure (i.e., who reports to whom, roles, and accountabilities), (2) systems (i.e., performance measures, business reviews), (3) shared values (i.e., beliefs, values, culture), and (4) skills (i.e., talents, knowledge). The elements all align with one another. The key message in this chapter is that *today's HR model (i.e., the integration of the four elements) continues to produce precisely what it was designed to produce when it was created in the 1960s.* HR's structure is the same, its measurement systems align beautifully to the structure, and the skills and shared values not only align with each other but to the structure and systems as well. When looking across the profession, rather than at any single company, the model fits together very well—the engine works. (See Figure 3-1.)

When the HR model was originally designed more than thirty years ago, it was expected to produce outputs for a personnel function. These included benefits policies, employee records, and payroll, as well as maintaining good labor relations to keep unions at bay. Take a look at

Figure 3-1. Today's HR model.

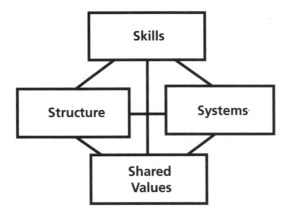

Figure 3-2, which shows two prototypical HR organizations separated by thirty years. The first organization is from the 1972 *Handbook of Modern Personnel Administration,*[2] which was the professional standard for many years. The second comes from a 2003 Corporate Leadership Council study of sixty-two HR organizations across twelve industries.[3] (Note: The percentages represent the percent of the sixty-two organizations with that department.)

Organizational titles have changed: Employment is now called staffing, personnel directors have become Chief Human Resources Officers, and personnel administrators became HR generalists and then strategic business partners. Despite these great titles, the daily activities and skills of HR business partners never have changed. HR departments (e.g., training, compensation) are changing their names to HR Centers of Excellence (COEs). Again, though, aside from the fancy title, little has changed.

Over the same thirty-year period, there have been dramatic changes in the results expected from the HR profession. There have been many articles written to help HR professionals deliver to these new expectations, but most have focused on training or tightening up today's model through increased accountability and additional performance measures.

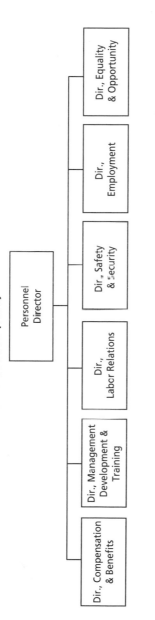

*Figure 3-2. A comparison of HR organizational structures from 1972 and 2003.*

**Handbook of Modern Personnel Administration (1972)**

Personnel Director

- Dir., Compensation & Benefits
- Dir., Management Development & Training
- Dir., Labor Relations
- Dir., Safety & Security
- Dir., Employment
- Dir., Equality & Opportunity

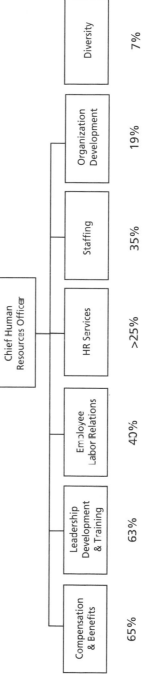

**Corporate Leadership Council Study of 62 HR Organizations (2003)**

Chief Human Resources Officer

- Compensation & Benefits — 65%
- Leadership Development & Training — 63%
- Employee Labor Relations — 40%
- HR Services — >25%
- Staffing — 35%
- Organization Development — 19%
- Diversity — 7%

In a July 2006 article in *Business Week*, Jack Welch states:

If there is anything we have learned over the past few years of traveling and talking to business groups, it is that HR rarely functions as it should. That's an outrage; made only more frustrating by the fact that leaders aren't scrambling to fix it. . . . HR should be every company's killer app.[4]

Welch goes on to suggest that the root of HR's problem is from the lack of accountability and measures. Two months later in September 2006, the *Harvard Business Review* published an article called "How to Fix HR." Its author, Gary Kaufman—much like Welch—chastised the profession for its pursuit of activities rather than results and for a lack of accountability. Peter Senge refers to this as the "Push Harder" paradigm. The underlying assumption is that the current model works just fine; the real problem is motivation, nothing that a good stiff push cannot fix. Yet if today's model for growing human capital is not designed to produce business results, stronger accountability— pushing harder—will not help.

Today's HR model was never designed to add value to customers or shareholders; it was designed to provide administrative services, to extricate managers from employee relations jams, and, at best, to provide support and advice. Many HR functions perform these functions well. However, today's HR model has not, does not, and will not produce business results through people until it is deliberately realigned for this purpose. You can hope that an ice cream machine begins to produce popcorn. You can complain about it, measure it, and angrily beat on it. But the machine will continue to produce precisely what it was designed to produce. Retitling machine bolts to be "strategic connectors" neither changes their function nor changes the output of the machine. HR can either shift to a new operational paradigm or retreat back to its original mission. Pushing harder on the ice cream machine will not produce popcorn.

## Today's Performance Gap

A performance gap is a gap between expectations and results. Today's HR is experiencing a performance gap. I do not mean to bash HR but to get us all on the same page. Every organizational change must begin with a clearly defined and commonly understood performance gap—the problem we are trying to fix. Let's first look at the gap from the perspective of those outside the profession and then again from those inside.

## A View from Outside the Profession

What outputs is HR being asked to deliver today? Accenture's 2004 High Performance Workforce Study surveyed CEOs to find out.[5] Results are displayed in Table 3-1. Notice how CEOs define their HR needs not as programs (e.g., rewards, training, succession planning) but as business results. Accenture not only found out what CEOs wanted but found that few were satisfied with their company's current performance on those key issues. For example, although improving worker productivity was seen by CEOs as the single most important HR initiative, only 6 percent—about nineteen out of twenty CEOs— reported being less than very satisfied with current performance. In fact, no more than 14 percent of CEOs reported being very satisfied with any of the five most important HR initiatives.

A more recent 2006 *Economist* survey found similar dissatisfaction.[6] The annual study surveyed 555 executives including 226 CEOs. When asked to identify the most critical corporate functions, respondents rated HR as tied for last with procurement and supply chain management. (See Table 3-2.)

*Table 3-1. Top five human resources initiatives
as defined by CEOs (ranked by importance).*

| INITIATIVE | PERCENT VERY SATISFIED WITH CURRENT PERFORMANCE |
|---|:---:|
| 1. Improving worker productivity | 6% |
| 2. Improving adaptability of the business to new opportunities | 11% |
| 3. Facilitating organizational change | 12% |
| 4. Improving employee engagement | 11% |
| 5. Improving delivery of HR services | 14% |

*Table 3-2. Main functional corporate roles*
*as identified by 555 executives.*

| FUNCTION | RELATIVE SCORE |
| --- | --- |
| Strategy and Business Development | 46 |
| Finance | 29 |
| Sales and Marketing | 25 |
| Risk | 14 |
| Customer Service | 12 |
| Information Technology | 10 |
| Operations and Production | 10 |
| Information and Research | 10 |
| R&D | 6 |
| Legal | 5 |
| Human Resources | 4 |
| Procurement | 4 |
| Supply Chain Management | 4 |

The same survey respondents rated HR as the poorest performing of all major corporate functions. In addition, few were confident that the profession is headed for better times ahead. (See Table 3-3.)

The data is unambiguous: In the majority of companies, HR is not a key player, its performance is the worst of all major functions, and line executives have little confidence that its value-add will change in the future. Maybe this is why USC's Center for Effective Organizations reported that approximately 25 percent of all Chief Human Resource Officer positions are filled with executives with no previous HR experience.[7] How many times have you heard of a company hiring a CFO with no finance background? The irony of the CHRO with no HR experience is that, according to the USC study, CHROs from outside the profession are less likely to be considered a business partner than those with HR backgrounds. Replacing a failing HR leader with a non-HR leader does not increase the business value of the profession.

Maybe we should simply write off strategic HR. However, when these same *Economist* survey respondents were asked for their biggest business challenges, human capital issues were prominent. (See Table 3-4, in which the HR topics are bold and italicized.)

*Table 3-3. Current and expected impact of HR
on business results, as reported by 555 executives.*

| "HOW DO YOU RATE THE PERFORMANCE OF YOUR BUSINESS IN THE FOLLOWING AREAS?" | "WHICH OF THE FOLLOWING BUSINESS FUNCTIONS WILL BE MOST IMPORTANT TO REALIZING YOUR CORPORATE STRATEGY OVER THE NEXT THREE YEARS?" |
|---|---|
| 1. Finance | 1. Sales and Marketing |
| 2. Customer Service | 2. Knowledge Management/Research |
| 3. Operations and Production | 3. Customer Service |
| 4. Sales and Marketing | 4. Operations and Production |
| 5. Risk Management | 5. Information Technology |
| 6. Knowledge Management/Research | 6. Risk Management |
| 7. Information Technology | 7. R&D |
| 8. Procurement | 8. Procurement/Sourcing |
| 9. R&D | 9. Finance |
| 10. Logistics | 10. HR |
| 11. HR | 11. Logistics |

It's tempting to write off HR and people issues, but given the importance of people and organizations to business success, that is not an option.

## A View from Inside the Profession

A view from inside the profession tells a similar story: HR has aspired to move into a strategic role, but it has not delivered on its aspiration. In a major longitudinal study conducted from 1995 to 2001, Edward

*Table 3-4. Greatest challenges to running a global company
over the next three years, as reported by 555 executives.*

| RISKS | RELATIVE SCORE |
|---|---|
| Understanding customers in multiple territories | 45 |
| *Managing teams effectively across borders* | 34 |
| *Finding high-quality people* | 31 |
| *Communicating a single strategic vision* | 29 |
| Building brands for multiple territories | 28 |

E. Lawler (the author of thirty-six books and more than 300 articles on people and organizations) and Susan A. Mohrman, both of the University of Southern California's Center for Effective Organizations, measured changes over time toward the vision of strategic HR. They found that despite large investments in outsourcing administrative tasks and investments in skill development, HR generalists (now called "business partners"):

- Had not changed in the percent of time spent in strategic versus administrative activities.

- Were not perceived as having improved their position as full partners who shape business strategy.

- Had not improved "business partner skills."[8]

In terms of HR's progress for delivering to its vision of business value, the authors concluded that:

> . . . the amount of change is surprisingly small. Given the tremendous amount of attention that has been given to the importance of HR being more of a value-added function, becoming a business and strategic partner, and adding value in a number of new ways, we frankly expected much more change.

## Why Is there a Performance Gap?

Data triangulated from very different sources and perspectives produces a consistent story: (1) People and organizational issues are critical for business performance, and (2) today's HR model does not deliver expected business results. Finding evidence of a performance gap is easy. Finding books or articles that define why the gap exists is very difficult.

Let's use the organizational capabilities model in Figure 3-3 to identify root causes of today's performance gap. This is a diagnostic tool that can be used to assess organization alignment in almost any organization. The left side of the model is the strategy side; we first need to know where we are going. We worked through the left side in Chapter 2 when we discussed the Human Capital Strategy, so the left-

*Figure 3-3. The organizational capabilities model.*

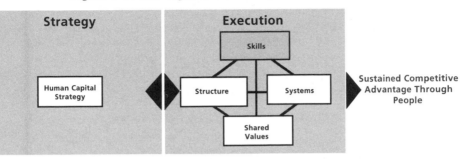

side is complete—we know what we want to accomplish. The right side of the model addresses execution of the strategy. We will define "today's HR model" as the sum of four organization elements: structure, systems, shared values, and skills. Each element must be explicitly designed to execute the Human Capital Strategy and must also be aligned with each of the other three elements.

Michael L. Tushman and Charles A. O'Reilly III wrote in *Winning Through Innovation*: "Incongruence, a lack of alignment or inconsistencies between [organizational] elements, is almost always at the root of today's performance gaps."[9] And so it is with HR. However, HR's incongruence is not within the four elements—those are well-aligned. It is between the right-side elements and the Human Capital Strategy. Table 3-5 summarizes the change taking place in the HR paradigm.

*Table 3-5. Summary of the HR paradigm change.*

| CURRENT PARADIGM | NEW PARADIGM |
|---|---|
| HR departments focused on administration and employee advocacy are failing on human capital growth tasks. | HR administration moved to Operations. Human capital organization aligned to improve human capital. |
| HR structure aligned by HR subprofession. | Human capital structure aligned to human capital strategic objectives. |
| HR measurements internally focused and activity-based. | HR measurements externally focused and results-based. |
| Internal customer satisfaction. | External customer satisfaction. |
| Retooled HR administrators. | Organizational change leaders. |

# Aligning the HR Structure

*The HR Structure Must Align with Business Results*

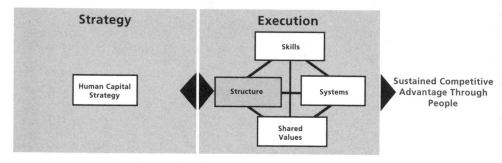

Today's HR organizational structure is misaligned with a Human Capital Strategy of sustained competitive advantage through people. There are two critical areas of misalignment:

1. Strategic and administrative work remains tangled.
2. HR is structured to produce HR products and processes rather than business results.

## Strategic and Administrative Work Remains Tangled

Several decades ago, sales and marketing organizations were commonplace. Over the years, marketing was split off into its own organization. Although the purpose of both functions is business development, each requires a different approach and skill set. The same is true with accounting and finance. Accounting is an old profession, and finance recently emerged from accounting with the rise of capital markets. The purpose of both functions is to leverage financial capital, but each uses different methods to accomplish the task. Like sales and marketing and accounting and finance, administrative and strategic HR are both about people, but each requires a different approach and skill set.

Over the past decades, the HR profession has aspired to create fundamentally different outcomes, but it has attempted to do so inside the walls of traditional HR. As the model presented in Clayton Christensen's *The Innovator's Dilemma* (Harvard Business School Press, 1997) would predict, it is difficult to create a business that represents a discontinuous change inside an old organization: The old will strangle the new. When an organization needs new capabilities, it may need a new organizational space where those capabilities can be developed.[10] Christensen suggests that a successful approach is to spin off an organization so that the new capabilities can be managed in a very different way than in the mainstream business. This has not happened in HR; the old is strangling the new.

The strategic HR seed was planted and nurtured in the traditional HR function, but it has failed to grow. It is time to press the reset button and start anew. Let's begin by defining three ways in which HR adds business value:

1. *The HR Administrator:* Handles employee records, benefits, compensation, payroll.

2. *The Fixer:* Fixes difficult situations, such as labor unions, quarreling executives, legal issues.

3. *The Strategic Partner:* Improves customer and shareholder satisfaction.

Each of the three roles is very important. Each role not only requires a different skill set but different talents. Skills can be developed over time, but talents cannot. Let's examine these roles using the following screens:

- Who is the customer? Where must the person focus?
- What education/experience is required?
- What talents/personality traits are required?

Then ask yourself: "How many people do I know who can be best-in-class in each of the three roles?" Should these roles be structurally separate? Is there a compelling reason to put these roles under the same roof?

**The HR Administrator.** The theory behind administrative HR is that fairness and consistency improve employee satisfaction, and satisfaction creates performance improvements. Good administrative HR professionals strengthen the perception of fairness by developing and enforcing consistent policies and processes. HR administrators do not, and should not, see themselves as accountable for improvements in external customer satisfaction or revenue growth. Since there is no tangible financial return on the investment for administrative activities, cost reduction is the key financial measure.

Successful HR administrators are service-oriented and process-oriented. They are comfortable with the stability and predictability. They are also good with detail, they value fairness and equity, and they enforce company policies. A 2006 Corporate Leadership Council Study found that "compliance expertise" is the HR profession's most accomplished skill.[11]

Taking on an administrative HR role does not require a specialist degree. Many non-HR members successfully transfer into HR administrative roles and can immediately perform standard duties such as managing the appraisal cycle or helping people with policy or benefit questions. Non-degreed HR professionals can learn HR policy and benefit programs as fast as degreed individuals.

**The Fixer.** The theory behind the fixer model is that improving employee relations is good for business. As David Newkirk, now CEO of executive education at the University of Virginia's Darden School of Business, stated:

> Every organization needs an HR person who can get senior managers out of tangled situations. These can include harassment cases, labor issues, etc. After years of pulling thorns out of the boss's paw, it is difficult to move the individual for not being a strategic contributor. Businesses need both individuals.[12]

He's right. Every executive needs a good fixer—someone to take care of the daily problems that distract an executive and place him/her in a role that is uncomfortable. Fixers provide advice and support to managers and executives and have strong negotiation skills. General managers often become deeply committed to their fixer. However, fixers contribute little to the development of sustained competitive advantage. Stamping our fires puts us back where we were in the first place.

**The Strategic Partner.** The theory behind strategic HR is that a company can win in the marketplace when its people outperform competitors' people. Strategic HR partners are accountable for driving business results through people and organizations—ensuring that the right people are in place, that jobs and organizations are properly aligned to the strategy, and that the work environment enables high performance. Successful strategic partners love change and hate bureaucracy. These folks have no desire to be compliance experts; in fact, in many ways, they are the antithesis of the HR administrator. Strategic partners focus externally on customers and shareholders. They see line managers as business partners, not customers. Strategic partners push line managers into unfamiliar territory. They debate, challenge, and argue, and they never accept a manager's diagnosis of people or organizational issues as "truth." The investment model for strategic HR is ROI-based.

Edward E. Lawler and Susan A. Mohrman of USC wrote about strategic partnering skills:

> Business-partnering effectiveness requires knowledge and skills in such areas as change management, strategic planning, and organizational design. These are complex judgmental areas where HR professionals have traditionally had little experience. This expertise is both hard to acquire and in short supply. Becoming expert in business partnering demands the acquisition not only of explicit knowledge, but also of tacit knowledge that comes from experience.[13]

Note that explicit knowledge comes from books and classes, while tacit knowledge is experiential.

Notice the differences in each of the three roles (HR administrator, fixer, and strategic partner). Each requires different skills, talents, and daily focus. Putting a single person in charge of all three ensures mediocrity. A 2005 *McKinsey Quarterly* article reported: "An effort to accomplish these complementary goals [strategic value-add and administrative cost reduction] with the same individuals, within the same career structures, and with the same HR leaders is almost bound to fail."[14]

Yet today's model commonly deploys a career path from administrative to strategic roles. After a person proves his/her value as a good administrator, the person becomes a candidate for an HR business partner opportunity. Given the differences in roles, one wonders if the best administrators will make the worst strategic business partners. No wonder today's business partner model has not worked. And neither accountability nor training will help.

## HR Is Structured to Produce Programs and Policies Rather than Business Results

Let's say, as a general manager, you see a leadership deficit in your business unit. Who in your HR function is accountable for improving leadership performance? The organizational development department is not; it creates competency models and assessment tools. The talent management department is not; it runs the succession planning cycle. The performance management department is responsible for appraisals, the compensation department makes pay decisions, and the training department develops and delivers courses. So which department manager will stand up and say, "My department is accountable for growing leaders"? Today, the answer is "nobody."

The reason is that today's HR is aligned by subprofession (e.g., training, staffing, compensation), the same as it was thirty years ago. Let's call these subprofessions by their new name, Centers of Excellence (COEs). COEs are factories that produce state-of-the-art HR tools. They are not designed to produce business results and often operate as uncoordinated product development units, as indicated by Figure 3-4, which shows the COEs of one institution.

Many companies refer to both first-level (e.g., organizational development) and second-level (e.g., HR metrics) organizations as COEs. If

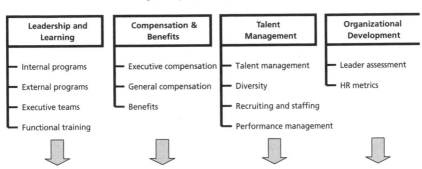

Figure 3-4. Centers of Excellence of a large
European financial institution.

this was an automobile engine, each COE unit would be producing a different engine part. The problem is that there is no blueprint of what the completed engine will look like or do. Just as it is unreasonable to build parts to an engine without a blueprint of the finished engine, it is unreasonable to build HR tools and processes without a Human Capital Strategy.

How, then, is COE performance evaluated today? Success is defined by external professional standards. For example, success is defined as world-class leadership development rather than as world-class leaders. Performance ratings depend on program quality and by volume of tools and products produced: a fat training catalogue, annual refreshing of the performance appraisal process, or a rich portfolio of recognition programs. More is better. That is why line managers so often complain about volumes of more "stuff" coming from HR. Good stuff, but to what end?

Today's COE design is based on the assumption that HR business partners will cobble together tools and programs from across COEs to build customized solutions for their business unit. This further assumes that two conditions exist: (1) Each COE has designed outputs to a common strategic plan, and (2) business partners have sufficient cobbling skills. What actually happens is that HR business partners end up being the equivalent of an auto assembly plant with Mercedes carburetors, Toyota rocker arms, and Chevrolet engine blocks. No amount of cobbling expertise can make up for parts that fundamentally do not fit.

A USC Center for Effective Organizations' study describes two prominent organizational characteristics of today's HR model: the decentralized generalist and the emergence of COEs. According to the study, COEs are designed to provide decentralized generalists with "sources of expert help." Has this model worked as intended? It has not. The authors summarize ten-year organizational changes in the HR profession:

> There is a significant *decrease* to which HR practices vary across business units. This finding suggests that while there may be dedicated HR leaders supporting businesses, their role is not to tailor HR practices to those businesses, but rather to work with centers of excellence and HR services teams to deliver common services to their parts of the organization.[15]

COEs are delivering results exactly opposite of what was intended. Rather than providing parts and advice to enable business partners to craft customized solutions, COEs are increasing the production and use of one-size-fits-all programs. The previously cited statistic that only 9 percent of HR leaders feel that human capital practices are connected to organizational performance is starting to make more sense. Once again: The problem is the HR model. It's broken.

## Realigning HR to Deliver Business Results

Two things will help us implement the new Human Capital Strategy by realigning HR to deliver business results: (1) splitting the HR administrator, fixer, and strategic partner roles, and (2) aligning the human capital organization to deliver the four strategic objectives.

**Split the HR Administrator, Fixer, and Strategic Partner Roles.** In 1964, Chaney and Owens conducted an academic study that makes a persuasive case that individuals with different personalities tend to migrate to jobs that fit. From a sample of 900, they looked back to high school and found that engineers disliked verbal activities and courses where discussion was involved, were slow in dating and preferred to spend time reading or in problem-solving activities. Those who became sales reps were only average in math and science capabilities, dated earlier, enjoyed meeting new people and had more friends and were leaders in different activities.[16]

Sure, there are some good "sales scientists," but not many, and trying to make a scientist into a sales rep may result in frustration by both parties. (As the saying goes, "Don't try to teach a pig to sing. It wastes your time and it frustrates the pig.") The study provides an important lesson for HR. The all-in-one HR business partner model has not and will not deliver value because it is based on an assumption that people can perform well in very different roles that require very different talents. It is time to admit defeat and completely separate the administrative, fixer, and strategic roles.

A more radical solution is to follow the *Innovator's Dilemma* model of creating a stand-alone unit for the discontinuous work of strategic HR. The head of HR administration should report to the corporation's top operations executive or CFO. This reporting relationship was very common in the days before the promise of strategic HR. It was common because it made sense. If the core capability of administrative HR is operational excellence, then operations is the right place to report. (See Figure 3-5.)

Next, build a fully separate organization reporting to the CEO that provides change leadership and organizational consulting to top leaders. Calling this organization something other than "human resources" might be wise as an HR title brings with it a set of internal customer service expectations that will no longer apply. This new "human capital" organization will comprise a set of full-time consultants who are educated and trained to improve the performance of people and organizations. Human capital business consultants should spend 100 percent of their time identifying opportunities to improve customer and shareholder satisfaction and should be evaluated by their impact to both.

*Figure 3-5. A new reporting relationship for HR, with administration reporting to operations.*

Their customer is external, their investment model is ROI-based, and they are business performance advocates.

**Align the Human Capital Organization to Deliver the Four Strategic Objectives.** To deliver business results, the human capital organization must align to the Human Capital Strategy. It must build and manage a system for delivering each of the strategic components: (1) effective executive teams, (2) leaders who deliver results, (3) key position excellence, and (4) workforce productivity.

Align corporate HR professionals to the strategic components (as shown in Chapter 1, in Figure 1-3), and make this dimension primary. Next, matrix COE members from their current professions to populate the new COE teams. For example, a compensation expert may be assigned to the workforce productivity COE. Each member remains aligned to a profession, and each profession continues to deliver on its value-added current tasks. For example, annual workforce plans would still be created and executed by the workforce management profession.

Members of the new COEs would be accountable for results that matter to customers and shareholders, as shown in Table 3-6.

To deliver the expected business results, each new COE will have several key duties:

- Set and execute a strategy to deliver the strategic objective.

- Engage the broader organization through personal leadership and influence.

*Table 3-6. Expected business results by COE.*

| COE | Main Performance Result |
|---|---|
| Executive Teams | Improve year-over-year performance results of senior leadership teams. |
| Leadership | Improve year-over-year performance of leaders. |
| | Effective allocation of leadership talent to key business and developmental opportunities. |
| Key Positions | Best-in-class industry performance for positions most critical to corporate core competencies. |
| Workforce Productivity | Best-in-class industry performance in workforce productivity. |

- Teach line managers to make effective human capital decisions.

- Measure and manage performance at individual and collective. levels to understand relationships and progress.

Most of these duties are probably self-evident. The third duty, teaching line managers to make good human capital decisions, may not be as clear. Think of the CFO model. No CFO can make all financial decisions, since maximizing return on financial assets requires scores of managers to make sound daily decisions. Many finance functions have helped managers make better financial decisions through formal training in basic finance. This same kind of training is required for managers to make more effective human capital decisions. Such training must be based on research in the behavioral sciences, particularly in organizational psychology and human learning. Managers should know how great leaders are most effectively developed, how competencies should be used (and not used), the most valid ways of predicting performance in new roles, and how best to motivate employees. The answers to these questions begin with behavioral science research, but they become far more powerful after company data has been captured and analyzed.

## Fixing HR Systems

*HR Systems Must Answer the Question: Does It Work?*

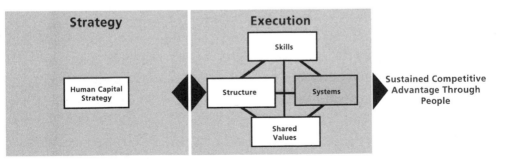

Systems refer to the controls an organization uses to measure, manage, and align the organization to a strategy or business plan. This section focuses on Human Capital Management systems: the current state and the required changes to create alignment with the new Human Capital Strategy.

## Today's Measurement Systems Measure Activities, not Results

Ask the leader of your organization's high-potential program, "Does it work?" and you might hear about "a new energy" in the air, attendance numbers, the portfolio of programs and workshops, or satisfaction ratings. But if the program was designed to accelerate the leadership performance of high potentials, "Did it work?" should mean, "Did the leadership performance of the high potentials improve?" You are likely to find that no one knows.

A Corporate Leadership Council (CLC) study of HR executives from 278 companies found that measurement is an increasingly important topic for HR:

- 87 percent of respondents saw HR measurement as important or very important.

- 93 percent felt that its importance will significantly increase over the next five years.

- 84 percent believed they would make significant increases in measurement investments over the next five years.[17]

Despite the perceived importance and a plethora of HR scorecards produced by HR consulting firms, only 20 percent of respondents felt that their current HR measurement systems were effective, and only one of the 278 felt it was very effective. The CLC study found that survey respondents see business results as the most important outcome of a measurement system but feel that today's measures are not achieving the goals of the system.

Why are today's measurement systems not producing the desired results? Because today's HR model uses a set of internally-focused, activity-based measures that logically align to today's HR structure, yet the business expects HR to add business value. Table 3-7 summarizes the results of CLC's benchmarking survey, which provides additional evidence that today's HR is well-aligned to a model that

*Table 3-7. The most commonly used HR measures.*

| MEASUREMENT CATEGORY | PROMINENT MEASURES | NON-PROMINENT MEASURES |
|---|---|---|
| HR Function | Total Operating Costs (71%, 84%) HR:FTE ratio (52%, 78%) HR Cost per Employee (54%, 50%) | Productivity of Individual HR Employees (45%, 17%) |
| Recruiting | Time to Fill (71%, 68%) New Employee Turnover (84%, 63%) Cost per Hire (74%, 60%) | Quality of Applicants (74%, 36%) New Hire Performance (75%, 26%) Employment Brand Strength (73%, 18%) |
| Training and Development | Satisfaction of participants (63%, 80%) Total training cost (74%, 71%) Number of employees who participated in training each year (60%, 63%) | Impact of training experiences on performance (88%, 24%) Individual manager track records for developing employees (80%, 13%) ROI of training (78%, 11%) |
| Compensation | N/A | N/A |
| Benefits | N/A | N/A |
| Organizational Effectiveness | Turnover by segment (87%, 87%) Employee satisfaction (81%, 79%) Number jobs filled internally (54%, 67%). | Gap between current and required skills (89%, 23%) Critical jobs occupied by below-average performers (74%, 12%) Employee Productivity (73%, 27%) |

does not meet today's expectations. The CLC research team aggregated sixty-one of the most common measures into categories and found the following:

- Measurement categories are aligned to today's subprofession-aligned HR organization.

- Measures most often used are internally focused and activity-based.

- Measures least often used are externally focused and results-based.

- Results-based measures are seen as more important than activity-based measures, but are used less.

In the second and third columns of the table, the first number in the parentheses is the percent who think the measure is important; the second number is the percent who use the measure. Thus, for example, for an HR Function measure like the HR:FTE ratio, 52 percent think it is important, but 78 percent use it—which means that some who do not think it is important use it anyway. Looking at non-prominent measures like the productivity of individual HR employees, we see that 45 percent think it is important, but only 17 percent capture that data.

The most prominently used measures are mostly internally focused and activity-based. These are measures that are unimportant to customers and shareholders. Does any customer of the Hilton Hotels care about total training costs or cost per hire? As for the non-prominent measures, they are all results-based. Do Hilton Hotel customers care about the quality of the store's new hires or the impact of training on employee performance? Absolutely. The HR respondents who completed the CLC survey believe that the results-based measures are more important than the activity-based measures, yet they use these measures much less frequently. They don't use them because results-based measures are misaligned with today's HR model.

## Measuring and Managing Human Capital Like Financial Capital

The data is clear: Today's HR measures are internally focused and activity-based. HR's new trend is to create measures that justify the existence of HR by evaluating ROI program-by-program. This is not a bad thing to do as long as the data is valid. When hard numbers are available, program-based ROI is useful. However, program-based ROI does not always work.

In the new paradigm, ROI calculations will be used when the data can be validated. The primary role is twofold: (1) to know if the performance of those in critical roles has improved year-over-year, and (2) to use experience to make progressively better human capital investment decisions. For example, we need to know not only whether leadership performance improved year-over-year; we also need to know why the change occurred in order to make better investment decisions next year.

When we understand the relative impact of each variable on leadership performance (a business result), we can learn from experience and progressively make better human capital decisions. For example, we might learn that certain types of training courses do not produce short-term or long-term gains. Or, we might learn that in the United States, the quickest way to improve performance is by managing out low performers, while in cultures such as Japan and France, separation costs may outweigh these gains. This knowledge helps COEs refine their points of view and continue to share the learnings with managers who make day-to-day human capital decisions. This is the antithesis to the one-size-fits-all trend happening today. This is what it means to measure and manage human capital with discipline.

By this point, you may feel that this conversation is still at too high a level. Hang on, because Chapters 4 through 7 delve deeply into each of the four strategic components of HCS. Each chapter includes advice on how to build measurement systems that enable the organization as a whole and managers as individuals to improve human capital decisions through collective experience.

## Shifting Values from the Internal to the External

*HR Shared Values Must Shift from an Internal Focus to an External Focus*

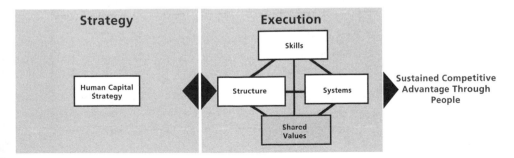

When Lou Gerstner entered IBM in 1993, he quickly came to realize IBM's problem was not the employees, who were very smart. It wasn't the brand or the technologies, either; both were world-class. IBM was failing fast because its culture could not adapt to changing business expectations. By the early 1990s, the market for computers was rapidly moving from corporate mainframe computing to PCs. New PC customers were just regular people using computers for word processing and adding up numbers—very different from computing department professionals who used complex computer languages to run mainframe applications. However, IBM's business model continued to produce the same output to the same customer set. Gerstner reported that in changing the business model, dealing with IBM's culture was the first, most important, and most difficult task.

Today's HR is in a very similar position. Almost all HR professionals understand the change of environment and the new business expectations, but most are locked into delivering expectations required by today's model. The glue that holds today's model in place is shared values, or HR's culture. As we have seen, today's HR professional is being pulled in very different directions: One direction is to align with today's model, while the other is to deliver business results. There are three cultural barriers that impede HR's ability to drive business results:

1. Internal versus external customer
2. The notion of "I can't own it; they don't report to me"
3. Activities versus results

**Internal Versus External Customer.** In the mid-1990s, when I was Director of Organizational Design for the McDonald's Corporation, a restaurant manager called and demanded that I conduct high school recruiting for her. When I suggested that this might be difficult, she said, "Look mister, I'm the customer and you'll do what I say!"

Who is HR's customer anyway? Today's customer is internal to the organization, so theoretically, the restaurant manager was right. Personnel was originally created to provide services to employees;

the department legitimately had an internal customer. HR still provides administrative services, and thus, it maintains that internal customer set. However, the new expectation of improving business performance through people is incompatible with an internal customer model.

In today's model, the HR generalist is called a "business partner." Think of the business partners of a small business. They are focused on the external customer and on business profits. Their talents and skills are, ideally, complementary, and they debate and challenge one another to surface the best option. Business partners win together and they lose together. Is it really possible to be a business partner to an internal customer?

**"I Can't Own It; They Don't Report to Me."** How many times has an HR partner said to a general manager, "I can't own it. You have to own it!"? That's true and that's false. The GM *does* have to own it. However, for the GM to own it, two conditions must exist: (1) The HR partner must have a solution that is sufficiently comprehensive and integrated to truly solve the problem, and (2) the HR partner must have sufficient influence skills to ensure that the GM and other influential leaders *share* ownership. Throwing a product over the fence to a GM with an attached note that says, "If it fails it's not my fault; you have to own it," is still too common a practice.

**Activities versus Results.** Gary Kaufman made a strong assertion about activities versus results in the September 2006 issue of the *Harvard Business Review*:

> Consider HR mission statements. Here's a typical one: "To provide quality services and support in hiring, training, staff relations, benefits, compensation, and safety beyond the expectations of all employees, enabling them to better serve our external customers." Shame on the managers who approved this slop! Statements like this are painfully short on real deliverables and accountability. Why? I suspect that senior managers don't understand what HR can deliver.[18]

**The Customer in the New Human Capital Strategy.** The single, most important leverage point for creating competitive advantage through people may be shifting from today's model of success as internal customer satisfaction to the new paradigm of external customer satisfaction. Here are four steps for defining a set of refreshed values for your human capital unit:

1.  Start at the top and work down.

2.  Insist on results.

3.  Take out those who do not add business value.

4.  Codify a new set of values.

Let's look at each of these steps.

**Start at the Top and Work Down.** The new human capital organization must begin with a clear statement of value, followed by a strategy for growing human capital, and finally, a plan to get there. As we discussed in Chapter 2, the vacuum created by the lack of a top-down plan is often filled by bottom-up approaches using best practice programs and tools. This is a fundamentally different mindset and approach. A top-down plan beginning with the business strategy or operational plan turns activity-based and product-based HR on its head.

**Insist on Results.** The key question to ask over and over is: "How is our HR work adding customer or shareholder value?" As mentioned at the beginning of this chapter, HR's role is *not* to be an adviser to businesspeople but to be the corporate leader for ensuring year-over-year human capital growth. Business results, not advice, is the goal.

When members of the human capital function are assessed by results, they stop worrying about who gets credit for what. When I worked in IBM Asia, our organization, Global Executive and Organizational Capability, committed to improve strategic management capabilities across Asia. To improve these capabilities, we created a Strategic Leadership Forum for IBM Japan, an organization of 20,000

IBMers. The forum brought together twenty-seven IBM industry teams (ten to fifteen members on each industry team), with representatives from software, services, hardware, consulting, etc., to create industry-based strategies (e.g., a strategy for selling IT solutions to banks or airlines). Our team worked the initial design, then engaged the IBM Japan Strategy team, who scheduled the event, chose the participants, and ran the forum. Few people ever knew our organization was involved.

We welcomed IBM Strategy's help, which enabled us to move on to the next forum with IBM China. Our team got credit for the quality of IBM Asia's strategies and completeness of execution, not for who ran each forum. Had we seen ourselves as accountable for activities, IBM Japan's strategy team would have been a competitive threat.

**Take Out Those Who Do Not Add Business Value.** John Sullivan, a professor at the University of San Francisco, calls for the immediate removal of those in HR who make the function less effective. He states:

> They have made it to the top by building relationships and playing politics, instead of producing measurable business results ( You can spot these [people] easily because they are always "in a meeting." They love meetings and think that going to a meeting is more beneficial than reviewing metrics, doing a post-mortem or forecasting people problems.[19]

You *must* take out these people to shift to a results-based culture. These individuals are often the most connected and influential members of the community, and their power will be most threatened by changes to a results-based paradigm. These individuals will be quickly exposed when given a task with a measurable business result.

**Codify a New Set of Values.** Write down the new values. Don't use ambiguous and politically correct terms such as "teamwork," "professionalism," and "integrity." Make each value unambiguous. Here are some examples from AT&T Global Services HR:

- "We are in charge of creating sustained competitive advantage through people. This means people in key positions will be better, in the eyes of our customers, than our competitors'."

- "We build and manage to an integrated model that systematically improves human capital. All HR methods will be integrated and aligned."

- "We manage to a full set of metrics that objectively demonstrates human capital improvement. We benchmark against competitors."

- "Our role is to be a business leader. 'The customer is the customer; HR is responsible for customer satisfaction.'"

## Using HR Skills to Provide Change Leadership

*HR Skills Must Provide Change Leadership*

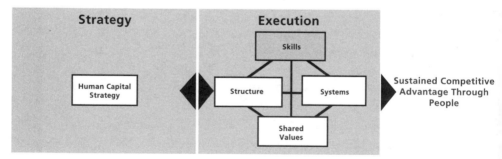

A 2003 study of line executives conducted by Lawler, Taylor, and Mohrman found that executives are only marginally satisfied with traditional HR services and even less satisfied with strategic HR support.[20] Table 3-8 provides a brief look at their findings.

If these were external customer satisfaction scores, the business would be in deep trouble. It is alarming to find that only 3 percent of customers are very satisfied with change management skills, and only 2 percent are very satisfied with organizational design skills. When

*Table 3-8. Marginal satisfaction with*
*HR services among line executives.*

| | PERCENT SATISFIED WITH HR SUPPORT | PERCENT VERY SATISFIED WITH HR SUPPORT |
|---|---|---|
| **Traditional HR** | | |
| • Functional HR Expertise | 53% | 25% |
| • Record Keeping | 51% | 13% |
| **Strategic HR** | | |
| • Business Understanding | 37% | 9% |
| • Organizational Design | 19% | 2% |
| • Change Management | 36% | 3% |

asked whether they are a true business partner, 79 percent of HR partners surveyed said they were, while only 53 percent of line executives surveyed felt the same way.

Lawler's team also asked HR business partners how their role has changed over the past five years. A large percentage reported that they spend more or much more time now than five years ago in strategic HR roles. (See Table 3-9.)

Notice how the majority of HR generalists reported an increase in strategic activities over time. However, when the research team looked at activity analysis data, they found that actual time spent on strategic HR activities had not changed in the seven years of the study. When the USC's Center for Effective Organization began its longitudinal study of HR in 1995, HR generalists reported spending 21.9 percent of their

*Table 3-9. Responses to the question: "How has the amount of*
*focus or attention to the following HR activities changed over the*
*past five to seven years as a proportion of overall HR activity?"*

| ACTIVITY | INCREASED | GREATLY INCREASED | TOTAL |
|---|---|---|---|
| Organizational Development | 42% | 28% | 70% |
| Organizational Design | 45% | 17% | 62% |
| Strategic Planning | 44% | 24% | 68% |
| Talent Assessment | 48% | 16% | 64% |

time in strategic activities.[21] A decade later, investments in strategic HR training and administrative process redesign and outsourcing increased that number to 23.5 percent—essentially, no improvement.

If you read HR literature, you will hear that too much administrative work is the most commonly cited reason for not doing strategic work. However, after many billions of dollars in administrative outsourcing and business process automation, time spent in strategic activities remains the same. Why? Because about the root of the problem is not administrative work. It is an organizational model that has locked HR into patterns of behavior misaligned with the needs of the business and the expectations of line executives. Administrators will continually find new ways to support internal customers.

There are several additional reasons that time spent as strategic partners has not improved. We discussed the first reason: Strategic partnering skill sets are misaligned with today's model. The student who attends strategic partner training returns to an administrative or fixer role with the same manager as before. We must change the model (i.e., the structure, measurement systems, and shared values) to strengthen the new skills before creating strategic business partner workshops.

The second reason strategic partnering has not improved is that few HR departments screen for capability to become a business partner. A recent Corporate Leadership Council survey found that only one-quarter of CHROs see their HR development activities as effective, and they see the most effective skill-building strategy as screening/recruiting rather than internal development.[22]

The HR shared value of fairness and equity requires that everybody have an opportunity to become a business partner. Just as it makes no sense to train me to be an NBA player, it is equally unlikely that many of today's HR generalists will ever become business partners. The roles of HR generalist and HR business partner require different talents, as shown in Table 3-10.

Research in behavioral science suggests that people can improve their "knowledge" with focused study. Skill, however, is a combination of knowledge and talent and is more difficult to improve than knowledge. Talent is largely innate—you are who you are. Unless a person's talents fit a given role, the person will never truly excel.

*Table 3-10. Contrasting talents of traditional and strategic business partner roles.*

| HR GENERALIST TALENTS | HR BUSINESS PARTNER TALENTS |
| --- | --- |
| Employee advocate—high affiliation motive | Customer and shareholder advocate—high achievement motive |
| Make people happy; likeable | Make people successful—push them out of their comfort zones; respected by line managers |
| Memorize and enforce policies; fairness and equity are key values | Hates bureaucracy; values meritocracy |
| Maintain equilibrium; "if it works, keep it" | Love to break things and build something better; "there's got to be a better way" |
| Executing ongoing programs to spec | Identifying opportunities for business improvement |

The third reason that today's development model does not work is that it is often based on a big knowledge-based event. Behavioral science research is clear; massed practice (i.e., learning in big chunks) is far inferior to distributed practice (i.e., learning in bite-sized chunks). You cannot develop strategic partnering skills in a two-week course. Consulting is a skill that requires ongoing, just-in-time development in the real world.

The fourth reason that today's development model does not work is that it is focused on the "who" rather than the "what." It is impractical, if not impossible, to change who a person is. It is very practical, however, to change what a person does. Too many competency models and associated training focus on being a "business partner" or a "change agent." Trainees return and wonder, "So, what do I do now?" Years of research in social psychology concluded that the best way to change who a person is to change what a person does.

**Replace Training with One-on-One Coaching.** One-on-one coaching may be the most powerful way to increase business partnering skills and build confidence and credibility. Long ago, I read a book on consulting that presented "The Law of Raspberry Jam," which stated "The more you spread it, the thinner it gets." So it is with book writing, classroom learning, and individual coaching: The broader you spread the word, the thinner it gets.

One-on-one advising and coaching is closely aligned to the following scientific principles of human learning: (1) distributed practice, (2) just-in-time learning, and (3) focusing on the "what."

Pure coaching can be conducted by a coach with little or no expertise. Coaching makes sense for those at advanced levels, but not for those at beginning or intermediate levels. Just as you cannot learn physics with a pure coaching model, you cannot learn strategic partnering either. For those with low competence levels, a just-in-time teaching model is a better choice than coaching. This requires that the teacher be an expert with a large toolbox and substantial personal experience. The coach will help the emerging business partner through critical tasks such as building and selling an annual human capital plan, building project plans and scorecards, and orchestrating large organization change.

**Outsource Strategic Roles.** For quick short-term gains, consider hiring contract-based organizational effectiveness professionals to take on strategic HR roles. There are a good number of independent consultants in organizational effectiveness who are available for hire. No leader wants to admit that he or she employs an army of consultants, but given the scarcity of qualified organizational effectiveness professionals and their tendency to move between organizations, this may be a logical move. Long-term contracting will reduce the consultant learning curve.

**Teach Newly Appointed Strategic HR Partners "What to Do" Rather than "Who to Be."** Through conferences, books, and articles, the HR profession has spent a huge amount of time discussing "who" the members will be, but the profession has not adequately specified what the profession will deliver or how it will get there. Experts use terms like "strategic adviser," "change manager," or "business partner" to define the "who," but they do not define the "what."

I have had an interesting time witnessing the aftermath of administrative outsourcing at several companies. HR business partners, now freed from administrative burdens, are very clear about who they need to be. However, they seldom know what to do when they come to work the next Monday morning. For example, how does the HR partner define and present business commitments to her general manager? How will she allocate her time during the day? What activities are required for change management leadership? In my experience, the most successful transformation of HR to a value-added function was when professionals new to the strategic role were initially told precisely what to do as well as why they are doing it. This is a prescriptive approach to development.

A prescriptive approach defines commitments and accountabilities. Does this sound like a cookbook approach? It is, but that is a reasonable place to begin. Here is a quick illustration:

*Accountability #1. Improve the effectiveness of executive leadership teams.*

- *Step 1:* Talk to the general manager about beginning an assessment of his/her executive team. Use the following discussion points. . . .
- *Step 2:* Interview each member of the executive team using the following interview guide. Take copious notes.
- *Step 3:* Read through all the notes, then ask, "What are the three most important themes I heard?" Then fill out the attached PowerPoint template to tell your story to the top team.

Don't train for competencies. Teach the HR business partners what to do. Start with a cookbook. If some business partners choose to use another version, that is okay.

## Conclusion

This chapter presented a diagnosis of why many organizations today need to realign their HR function to execute a Human Capital Strategy. The data is compelling: Today's HR model was designed to produce outputs for a personnel function. The model has changed little over the past decades even though the expectations for HR have changed dramatically.

The *Innovator's Dilemma* model suggests that the necessary changes require new skills, values, and measurements. Such changes are difficult under the umbrella of the current organization. Not only has strategic HR been under the same umbrella with administrative and employee relations units, but HR business partners have been required to run all organizational models simultaneously. The HR function simultaneously embraces several different theories: HR as the keeper of fairness and consistency (the HR administrator), HR as protector of employees (the HR fixer), and HR as driver of profit and customer satisfaction through people (the HR strategic business partner). These diverse assumption sets have confused a most basic question: "Who is the customer?" Is the line manager the customer, or is the line manager a business partner with whom HR works to address the needs of an external customer?

Continual improvements have been used for decades to align the traditional HR model to the new value-added vision. However, this new vision represents a discontinuous shift and requires following the principles of discontinuous organizational change. These include creating an autonomous organization and explicitly realigning values, measurements, and skills. This chapter has presented an approach for creating this realignment.

# Notes

1. C. Christensen and S. Kaufman, "Assessing Your Organization's Capabilities: Resources, Processes & Priorities" (unpublished paper).

2. D. Campbell, "The Personnel Director, his Staff, and the Structure of the Department," in J. Famularo, ed., *Handbook of Modern Personnel Administration* (New York: McGraw-Hill, 1972), pp. 4–10.

3. Corporate Leadership Council. *HR Organization Profiles: Structures of the Human Resources Function* (Washington, D.C. Corporate Executive Board: June, 2003).

4. J. Welch and S. Welch, "*So Many CEOs Get This Wrong,*" *Business Week* (June 2006).

5. Accenture, "Accenture High Performance Workforce Study," p. 8 (2004). Accessed on www.accenture.com (April 6, 2007).

6. *CEO Briefing: Corporate Priorities for 2006 and Beyond,* Economist Intelligence Unit (2006).

7. E. Lawler and S. Mohrman, "HR as a Strategic Partner: What Does It Take to Make It Happen?" *Human Resource Planning,* Vol. 26 (2003).

8. E. Lawler and S. Mohrman, *Creating a Strategic Human Resources Organization: An Assessment of Trends and New Directions* (Stanford, Calif.: Stanford University Press, 2003).

9. M. Tushman and C. O'Reilly, *Winning Through Innovation* (Boston: Harvard Business School Press, 2001), p. 58.

10. C. Christensen and M. Overdorf, "Meeting the Challenge of Disruptive Change," *Harvard Business Review* (March–April 2000).

11. Corporate Leadership Council, *Defining Critical Skills of the Human Resources Staff* (Washington, D.C.: Corporate Executive Board, 2006), p. 13.

12. Personal conversation with David Newkirk, CEO of University of Virginia, Darden School's Executive Education program, April 24, 2007.

13. E. Lawler and S. Mohrman, *Creating a Strategic Human Resources Organization: An Assessment of Trends and New Directions.*

14. E. Lawson, J. Mueller-Oerlinghausen, and J. Shearn, "A Dearth of HR Talent," *McKinsey Quarterly,* Number 2 (2005).

15. E. Lawler, J. Boudreau, and S. Mohrman, *Achieving Strategic Excellence: An Assessment of Human Resource Organizations* (Stanford, Calif.: Stanford University Press, 2006).

16. F. Chaney and W. Owens, "Life history antecedents of sales, research and general engineering interest," *Journal of Applied Psychology,* 60, pp. 767–769.

17. Corporate Leadership Council, *Exploring the Measurement Challenge. Results of a Membership Survey on HR Metrics* (Washington, D.C.: Corporate Executive Board, Fall 2001).

18. G. Kaufman, "How to Fix HR," *Harvard Business Review* (September 2006).

19. J. Sullivan, "Vipers in your Midst," *Workforce Management,* Vol. 85, No. 16 (2006).

20. E. Lawler and S. Mohrman, *Creating a Strategic Human Resources Organization.*

21. Ibid.

22. Corporate Leadership Council (2006), p. 16.

*Part Two*

# BUILDING

# THE

# SYSTEM

# Chapter Four

# Effective Executive Teams

*"Are your executive teams more effective this year than last year?"*

A large business unit of a European technology company was failing. Product yield problems had created product shortages and angry customers. Steve, one of the most talented and highly respected scientists in the industry, was the general manager of the unit. Not only did Steve possess extraordinary technical capabilities, but he was a sharp businessman. He was powerfully smart, more so than the vice presidents who reported to him. He knew it and they knew it.

When answers to difficult questions did not come quickly to others, Steve answered them easily. He could always find a flaw in a presentation or an argument. Intellectual sparing produced incremental boosts in Steve's ego and incremental drops in the confidence of his vice presidents. Steve enjoyed being right. Of course, he wasn't always right, but even when he wasn't, it seemed as though he was.

Over time, the distance between Steve and his vice presidents increased and reality-based conversations ceased. Steve made customer commitments that his direct reports and their organizational members knew were not possible, but arguing was futile and the business missed product volume commitments month after month. Steve's vice presidents were caught in a situation with no chance of a positive outcome: They could not make volume commitments, but neither could they change the numbers. Members of each vice president's department from top to bottom vainly looked up to their immediate supervisor to reestablish reasonable product commitments. Losing was assured for virtually everyone, and with each loss came a new round of budget cuts. The business was soon swamped in red ink, and its most important customer made a publicly embarrassing switch to a competitor.

I learned one of my most poignant lessons of leadership watching Steve. The unit's failure was not caused by technology or employee quality; both were among the industry's best. Instead, failure was caused by a single leader who could not effectively lead an executive team; this person triggered a performance collapse of an organization of almost 20,000 people. When I figured this out, I came to the realization that no amount of good work at the bottom matters if the top isn't right.

Getting the top right requires shifting the paradigm for improving executive team performance. Many books and articles today approach executive teaming from a bottoms-up, program-based perspective. These writings are rich with tools and techniques for building trust, establishing effective meeting protocols, etc. It is not that these activities are unimportant. They certainly are important. However, performance improvements require a top-down approach, one that begins by defining the outputs of the executive team. Approaching executive teaming from the top-down approach is the fundamental shift required for teams to improve their business contribution.

## Why Are Executive Teams Important?

It is tough being a general manager. As competitors proliferate and business operations expand around the world, the role of the general manager has become increasingly complex. A 2006 study from the National Bureau of Economic Research found that CEO turnover for publicly traded U.S. *Fortune 500* companies is up from 12 percent in 1992 to 18 percent in 2005.[1] Surprisingly, the most common reasons for dismissal are not related to financial performance. In another study of 1,087 board members of 286 organizations found that CEOs do not get fired for missing financial numbers but for losing the confidence of board members that they can build an organization capable of producing reliable returns in the future.[2] This sounds a lot like the *Good to Great* findings cited in Chapter 2, and a lot like the central theme of this book.

It may be possible for a smart CEO to make good financial or strategic decisions with minimal support from others in the organization. However, it is not possible for a CEO to build organizational capabilities alone. More and more, today's best-performing corporations are moving toward integrated executive teams to provide day-to-day leadership for the overall organization.

Executive teams include the leaders of a company's business units, regions, countries, or functions. These are the ongoing teams that lead an organizational unit and are accountable for the unit's business results.

## Building the Executive Team

A few years back, I was working with Mike Cadigan, the general manager of IBM Semiconductor, and his executive team. Mike said, "Hey, Brad, we've been spending a lot of time working on this team. Are we better than when we began this journey?" I had no idea. In fact, I did not even know what "better" meant. I had been pursuing a bottoms-up approach to executive team development. We had been working diligently on the "how" without ever defining the "what." We had run a number of different sessions: a strategy development session, a session where we discussed team and individual roles, a session where we set meeting times and standard agendas. But we had never stopped to ask the most important questions:

- What must this team deliver to the business?

- What are the three to five things the team must do extraordinarily well to achieve those results?

- How will the team focus and discipline its efforts and measure and manage its progress?

I had unconsciously defined success as team characteristics—trust, effective meetings, and so on—rather than team results. We needed to turn our approach on its head and start with business results. Only after the team defines its purpose, its outputs, and the most important things to get right should we begin thinking about characteristics, programs, and activities.

This purpose of this chapter is to convince you to fundamentally change your approach for improving executive team performance from a bottoms-up, internally focused, activity-based approach to a top-down, externally focused, results-based one. Success is being able to report to the CEO the year-over-year performance changes of his/her executive teams, where the changes occurred, and why they occurred.

This chapter is divided into two main sections. The first section describes a high-level, top-down approach for building executive teams that consistently deliver results that matter to shareholders, customers, and people. The second section is a roadmap for building a system for measuring and managing executive teams to deliver those results. Let's start with executive team design.

## Executive Team Design

Designing a high-performance executive team is a top-down process that begins by defining the purpose of the team and ends with agreement on how the team will operate to deliver those results. Figure 4-1 presents a five-step process for designing the team.

*Figure 4-1. A top-down approach for designing executive teams.*

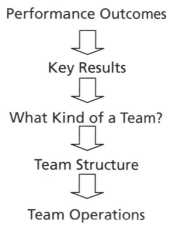

Performance Outcomes

⬇

Key Results

⬇

What Kind of a Team?

⬇

Team Structure

⬇

Team Operations

## Performance Outcomes

The purpose of most ongoing executive teams is to "lead the organization." The core mission of the executive team is to translate that abstract challenge into a clear set of team goals, subgoals, and work projects that improve business performance. When this important step is missed, executive teams end up "operating" without a common goal or priority set. We have all seen leadership

teams that missed this step. They spend the bulk of their meeting time chasing urgent issues or obsessing about the past week's financial results. Certainly, coordination around urgent issues will always be required; however, members of a high-performing team have stated agreements about which urgent issues are appropriate for team discussion (rather than being settled at lower levels), and at which meetings such discussion is appropriate. Great executive teams manage the business rather than letting the business manage them.

Managing the business begins with an end-state measure of success. Let's refer to this lagging indicator as the *performance outcome*. Performance outcomes are most often expressed as financial, operational, or customer satisfaction measures. The first task for every executive team is to define the performance outcome and measure(s) of success. Performance outcomes must be sufficiently clear that all organizational members know whether the business is winning or losing.

## Key Results

Once performance outcomes are set, the next question to address is: "What, specifically, must this team do to achieve the performance outcomes?" While this may seem obvious, even in the best executive teams, members often have not precisely stated what the team must do to deliver the business plan. Recently, I asked eight executives in the top team of a business unit to list the team's five highest priorities.

Performance Outcomes

**Key Results**

What Kind of a Team?

Team Structure

Team Operations

The members listed nineteen priorities, yet only one priority appeared on every executive's list. Although team members cited the same performance outcomes, they were not in agreement on the most important results to deliver those outcomes.

When leading indicators are not set, teams manage to lagging indicators and struggle to develop the organizational capabilities required to produce reliable future results. Since the team has not defined the most important leading indicators, their time together will be scattered across urgent issues. Let's call these leading indicators the *key results*. Why use the word "result"? Because these are not competencies (i.e., things the team is able to do) or activities (i.e., things that the team does). Instead, these are the most important things the team must accomplish to deliver the performance outcomes. In his book *First Things First* (Simon & Schuster, 1994), Stephen R. Covey writes about putting rocks in a jar. He says that you can fit more rocks in a jar if you put the big rocks (the most important tasks) in first and then fill in with the pebbles (the less important activities). Key results are the big rocks.

Figure 4-2 is a visual depiction of leading and lagging indicators. In this example, the performance outcome is service revenue growth, which is a financial measure. To achieve this outcome, the team has decided they must deliver four key results—alliance effectiveness, solution selling

*Figure 4-2. An example of performance outcomes and key results.*

capabilities, organizational realignment, and product development. Theoretically, if the team delivers excellent performance on all four key results, service revenue will grow. The core task of the executive team is to ensure performance excellence on each of the four results. In this way, the new HCS largely *measures* performance on lagging indicators, but *manages* performance by leading indicators. When leading indicators are correctly designed and performance on each improves, financial and operational results will follow.

Managing to key results not only helps the executive team become more efficient and effective in delivering its stated performance outcomes. It also:

- Increases trust levels between members and reduce politicking.
- Reduces time spent looking backward.
- Enhances the team's ability to learn from experience.

**Key Results and Trust.** On a past consulting project, I worked with the president of the China subsidiary of a U.S. company. He called me after a survey of his executive team members indicated that team members did not trust one another. How could it be, he wondered, that the members of a group who had worked together for more than a decade did not trust one another? It took only a few interviews for the cause to became clear: Executive team members viewed the team's purpose and priorities very differently. A rational decision for one executive was seen as irrational and self-serving when viewed from a different set of assumptions. This was not an interpersonal problem at all. Trust problems were merely a symptom; a misaligned assumption set was the root cause.

**Key Results and Backward-Looking Management.** Long-term performance suffers when executive teams spend the bulk of their time looking backward in the rearview mirror. We have all sat in executive team meetings where the leader knows that he will have to explain last week's numbers to the boss, so he spends the bulk of the meeting time trying to "spin" a message. Yet when sales cycles are long—let's say, ten to twelve months—it makes little sense to look for last week's causes for last week's sales shortfalls. Last week's shortfalls were caused by last year's decisions.

**Key Results and Team Learning.** Managing by lagging indicators makes it difficult for executive teams to learn from experience. Cause-and-effect relationships are unclear, and even when they are known, the feedback loop is too long for effective learning. Peter Senge of MIT uses a metaphor of trying to properly adjust shower temperature by turning the hot and cold water faucets. A person jumps into a cold shower and turns the hot water higher and higher until suddenly, the water is scalding. At that point, the person quickly turns down the hot water, but goes too far and gets a blast of cold water. Managing by lagging indicators is similar. Even if the team is able to isolate a root cause, after a delay of six to twelve months, the environment will have changed. Turning the faucet hard now will likely create a new problem that will not be known until the following year.

Managing to leading indicators shortens the feedback cycle and enables the team to understand relationships between decisions and results. The shorter the time between decisions and feedback, the more rapid the learning. Let's face it: Even in good executive teams, about one-third of the decisions will be good, one-third will be fair, and one-third will be bad. High-performing executive teams monitor the effectiveness of their decisions. They learn from their good decisions and fix those that were bad. Year-over-year improvements in executive team performance requires a formal, disciplined process for feedback and learning.

## What Kind of a Team?

Deciding what kind of executive team is needed follows an agreement on key results. The choice of an optimal teaming approach is largely a function of the degree to which:

Performance Outcomes

⇩

Key Results

⇩

**What Kind of a Team?**

⇩

Team Structure

⇩

Team Operations

- Team members have common goals.

- Tasks are interdependent and require coordination.

- The work requires different skills and perspectives.

Have you ever been on a team where your work was not really aligned with other team members' work? The cost of being on the team was clear, but you might have wondered how this team added value to you or to the business. Too often, managers form direct reports into a team because of organizational relationships rather than to address a specific business need. Having a common supervisor is not a sufficient condition for forming a group of individuals into a team. How, then, should teams be designed?

The choice of a team design depends on the desired performance outcome. The design must balance the costs of teaming with the expected impact on the performance outcomes. Teaming costs include time spent in executive team meetings or on subprojects as well as ongoing investments in relationships with other team members. When team members feel that teaming costs exceed benefits, they become frustrated and disillusioned and send the team into a downward performance spiral.

**Real Teams and Working Groups.** The two most common types of executive teams are real teams and working groups. A *real team* operates like a small musical ensemble. The output of the ensemble is one unique sound—a collective work product. The team does its work together, leadership is shared, members are accountable to one another, and the team wins or loses together.

*Working groups* are different. In working groups, individuals are the primary focal point for performance results. Working groups require a strong, focused leader who ensures that work products are integrated and coordinated. The performance contract is between the team leader and each team member rather than between team members. Team member performance expectations are aligned to their assigned responsibilities and work products, and individual outputs are aggregated to create a final team product. Figure 4-3 illustrates the differences between real teams and working groups.

**Real Teams and Working Groups: Two Case Studies.** In the mid-1990s, Taco Bell redesigned its store openings process. (This was a subproject of the larger initiative presented in Chapter 2.) The team assigned to the project was designed as a real team model that brought together four members—one each from finance, marketing, construction, and human resources—to jointly build a store opening process from the perspective of the new store manager rather than from headquarter departments. The team developed a step-by-step roadmap that radically reduced cycle time, improved store opening quality, and provided a feedback loop that enabled the corporation to use its collective learnings to continually improve future store openings.

At the same time, one of Taco Bell's competitors chose to open 250 units in Southern California over a three-month time period.

*Figure 4-3. Real teams versus working groups.*

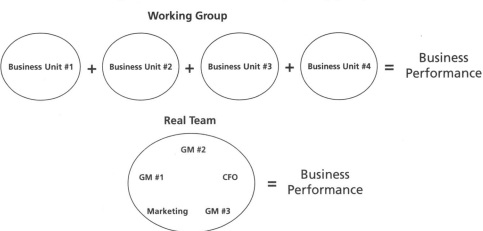

Rather than using the real team approach, this company chose the working group approach. Its project was launched with several hundred employees and managers grouped by departments in a theater-style room. The meeting organizer announced the goal and asked each department to sharpen its pencils and come back with an accelerated plan (following the "Push Harder" paradigm referred to in Chapter 3). Given that this was a significantly bigger challenge than the company had ever taken on before, the company's choice of the department-centric working group approach led to only incremental improvements in store opening speed and quality. In the end, incremental improvements were not sufficient to the challenge. The company did not deliver its units on time, and opening performance was much worse than average.

These cases are not presented to suggest that real teams are always the most effective teaming model. It depends on the circumstance. When breakthrough performance is required, the advantage goes to the real team model. However, normal business operations do not require daily breakthroughs. This is why working groups are most commonly used for executive teams—they fit the primary task of leading the organization. When performance breakthroughs are needed, the working group model is inadequate. The answer is to leverage the benefits of working groups *and* real teams by using the working group model as the base operating model and creating part-time real teams to create breakthrough performance in areas that are most critical to business success.

## Team Structure

Few would disagree that a good team leader is essential for team performance, but what is good team leadership? A good team leader ensures that the team reliably achieves its stated performance outcomes. Research on executive teams seems to coalesce around four leadership results that a team leader must deliver for the team to achieve its outcomes:

Performance Outcomes

Key Results

What Kind of a Team?

**Team Structure**

Team Operations

1. Clear team purpose
2. Right team structure and skills
3. Committed and confident members
4. Mutual accountability

Notice again that these are not stated as competencies. They are results that can, and should, be measured at regularly defined intervals.

**Clear Team Purpose.** The most important leadership result is a team purpose that is known and accepted by each member. A good way to assess the current level of clarity is to ask each team member the following questions individually: Do team members express the team's challenge in the same way? Does each describe performance outcomes and key results in the same way?

**Right Team Structure and Skills.** This means that all the skills needed to deliver the plan are represented on the team. That may not be the case. On many executive teams, membership is defined by organizational position. ("Kathy is one of my direct reports, so she needs to be on the team.") Although excluding a direct report may be politically difficult, it is more important that the team is staffed with the right skills. Choose only members who will truly add value. There may be hurt feelings, but you must consider the trade-off for team performance. In addition, if a critical skill is not represented by those on the organizational chart, the team leader must find and include that skill as well even if doing so seems politically awkward at first.

**Committed and Confident Members.** The third result the team leader must deliver is team members who are deeply committed to the team's purpose and defined outputs. When executive team members are not committed, people both inside and outside the executive team know. Commitment is influenced by confidence that the team can, and is, adding value to the business. Little wins and celebrations create momentum, learning, and confidence to take on progressively larger challenges.

**Mutual Accountability.** Finally, the leader must create a team environment that encourages mutual accountability. Think of any great sports program. Team members routinely hold one another accountable for delivering exceptional results. This mutual accountability shifts the burden of performance management from the leader to fellow members, who are usually less forgiving of performance shortfalls than the team leader him/herself. Mutual accountability creates and sustains team energy without the leader having to infuse energy into the team.

## Team Operations

Team operations are where most consultants propose and most writings begin. In a top-down approach, operations should be addressed last. Here are a few practices for improving the operations of executive teams:

Performance Outcomes

⇩

Key Results

⇩

What Kind of a Team?

⇩

Team Structure

⇩

**Team Operations**

- Decide when and why the team will meet.
- Set team norms.
- Create meeting protocols.

**Decide When and Why the Team Will Meet.** Consider a zero-based approach to setting executive team meetings. If the preceding steps were thorough, team member assumptions will be aligned and members will make good decisions on: (1) what meetings are needed to fully deliver to expectations, (2) the purpose for each meeting, (3) how long each meeting will be, (4) who will attend, and (5) the base agenda. It is also helpful to decide what each meeting will *not* be—what agenda items will not be allowed, who will not be invited, etc.

I have seen a number of effective practices for setting executive team meetings. The first is to hold executive team meetings in different locations. That way, the day before the meeting, executive team members can meet with customers, suppliers, and employees in the location to better understand the local business environment and to create closer ties between employees and high-level leaders.

Another effective practice is to hold strategy and organizational capability meetings separate from operational meetings. When both topics are addressed as separate agenda items in the same meeting, the "tyranny of the urgent" crowds out strategic and capability improvement discussions. Too often, then, strategic discussions are pushed to the afternoon of the last day, when members are tired and begin leaving one by one to catch flights home. A more effective method is to schedule operational updates once a week for an hour or two. Operational reviews must be timely to add value. Strategic and capability improvement meetings are not as time sensitive and do not necessitate such short intervals. These can be scheduled monthly or even quarterly, so that team members can thoughtfully think, debate, and discuss to continually expose reality, align assumption sets, and rethink operational paradigms. These meetings typically require one- or two-day sessions.

**Set Team Norms.** Team norms are agreements by team members of how the team will operate. (Some may use the less clinical term "rules of the road.") It is helpful to post these agreements during team meetings and encourage members to good-naturedly catch violators. Figure 4-4 presents an example from a senior executive team.

**Create Meeting Protocols.** Consider creating a base agenda for each meeting. Decide which agenda topics need to be reviewed every time—

*Figure 4-4. An example of executive team norms.*

**Always Do**
- Attend in body and in action. Active participation in all meetings.
- Seek first to understand and then to be understood.
- Stick to the agenda, stay on topic, bring facts, allow time for discussion.
- Model the way; lead by example.
- Make decisions based on facts and execute.

**Never Do**
- Never behave in ways that are disrespectful to members.
- No e-mail or phones.
- Absences must be explained to team members.
- Leave self-interests at the door. Think about the broader team agenda.

for example, progress to defined milestones, performance measures, follow-up from last meeting assignments, and team member recognition. Effective meeting protocols also define the data to be brought to each meeting and the way decisions will be made in the meeting.

In some companies, the executive meeting is a forum for putting issues on the table and debating them to surface truth. In my experience, this approach fits well in cultures like the United States and Australia. However, in Japan and many European countries, executive meetings tend to be formal approval forums for decisions that have been made earlier in one-on-one discussions. Having executive team members discuss the merits of each approach and consciously choose the one they will use for each meeting will improve team performance.

## Improving Executive Team Performance: A Roadmap

So far, this chapter has presented a high-level approach to building an effective executive team. Think of this as a description of success in regard to the structural aspects of the team. The next section presents instructions for making the changes. The following topics are covered:

- How to define performance outcomes (i.e., lagging indicators)
- How to define key results (i.e., leading indicators)
- How to build a system for effectively measuring and managing key results

### How to Define Performance Outcomes

Let's begin with step #1: clarifying the expected business results. Defining the business unit's commitments should not be terribly difficult; these come from above and are expressed by lagging indicators of financial, market share, operational, or customer results. The challenge is not to find business result metrics; it is to edit the results down from what looks more like a Boeing 747 dashboard to a performance scorecard. Too many metrics is no better than no metrics.

Simplifying and focusing is a mark of great leadership. Mike Cadigan of IBM Semiconductors realized that the piles of metrics in his organization really were in support of one main thing to get right. The business needed to "keep the fabrication plant (fab) full." Most new fabrication plants are assets worth more than a billion dollars. Keep the fab full and you make money; if not, you lose money. Sales, marketing, partnerships, and joint ventures had one purpose: to keep a steady flow of orders to the fab. Once the theme of "fill the fab" was set, then finance, HR, communications, and strategy functions were required to state explicitly how their objectives, plans, and results helped fill the fab. If they were not focused on that goal, they were creating drag. Great leaders simply identify the challenge and focus large numbers of people on that challenge.

Cadigan's top team at IBM Semiconductor then created a scorecard of the measures with the greatest impact on keeping a steady flow of orders to the fab. The scorecard enabled team members to discuss, debate, and analyze the most critical leading indicators and then define the relationships between each.

Defining the performance outcomes for each executive team is a critical first step. The team may choose one of several outcomes (financial, operational, and customer), or members may choose to combine all three to a weighted performance index—a single number that defines a win or a loss. In virtually all sporting events, there is a single performance outcome. The athlete/team either wins or loses; the athlete/team never wins on two measures and loses on a third. Yet often in year-end town hall meetings, business executives cherry-pick results to highlight while the audience wonders: "Did we win or did we lose?"

A completed scorecard is a valuable output of executive team discussions; however, there is equal value in the debate itself as diverse assumption sets begin to converge. For example, the marketing leader might feel that customer satisfaction is the primary success measure and that sales excellence is the leverage point. Sales might see profitability as the most important measure and manufacturing quality as the leverage point. Manufacturing might agree that profitability is most important but feels that profitability is most related to quality and that having sales sell standard products is the leverage point.

Surfacing and working to converge assumption sets requires expert facilitation and hard data. A facilitator might ask questions such as:

- If net profit is our key financial measure, should we continue to manage market share?

- What is the relationship between market share and net profit?

- Which measures of customer satisfaction are most important for driving net profit growth?

Success is when each member describes the team's performance challenges and business commitments in the same way. If executive team members cannot do this, it is unlikely that organizational members beneath will be able to do so. A Gallup organization study of 80,000 employees found that the most important leadership result is to ensure that employees know what is expected of them.[3] Many other studies have confirmed Gallup's finding that role clarity is the most important driver of human capital productivity. Sharpening up the business challenges and priorities among those at the top is the first step in driving clarity down the organization and producing real shareholder value.

Spending several days away from the office to hold these important discussions will be time well spent. The discussion will proceed more smoothly if finance and market research folks attend and are able to present statistical relationships between variables; this helps the team move from opinion to facts. For example, the data might show that every one percentage point in customer satisfaction is worth a .3 percent change in revenue growth, but there is a six-month lag from the customer satisfaction change to revenue realization.

Consider sending the following materials several weeks before the meeting:

- The decisions to be made

- The five to ten questions the team will discuss

- Key analyses generated by functional organizations that best describe their view of the business (for example, finance might show the most important predictors of share price or profitability)

Ask team members to solicit thoughts and perspectives from people throughout their organization. The more broad and diverse the perspectives, the better the outcome.

## How to Define Key Results

Once performance outcomes are set and underlying assumptions are aligned, the next task is to determine the three to five key results (i.e., leading indicators) that the executive team must deliver to achieve the stated business results. The process for setting key results is similar to the one above for defining performance outcomes. This again provides an opportunity for team members to surface and debate assumptions until they coalesce into a shared and documented team assumption set.

There is no "one best model" for an executive team that ensures that it will achieve its key results. The best model is the one that enables a particular team to reach its stated performance outcomes. The chosen model must take into account the performance outcomes, the business environment, and the current capabilities of the team. Here are few examples of executive teaming models.

**Model #1: Help a New Team Coalesce.** This model is helpful for executive teams that are in the beginning stages of development. The model shown in Table 4-1 was populated by team members when the team looked at itself and decided that there were four things it needed to do better to become a higher performing team. Notice that the team used both objective and subjective measures to measure and manage their performance.

**Model #2: Manage for In-Year Performance.** This model is directly aligned to delivering the in-year business plan by answering the question: "Given our performance outcomes and business strategy, what are the three to five strategic objectives that we must deliver in the next twelve to twenty-four months?" Think of these as results that matter to customers and/or shareholders rather than as internal things to get

Table 4-1. A behaviorally based executive team model.

| Key Results | Phase 1: Structure and Operations | Phase 2: Gaining Traction | Phase 3: Perpetual Motion | Measure |
|---|---|---|---|---|
| Strategic Clarity and Interlock | Business strategy set and operationalized<br>Priorities clearly articulated by each team member<br>Individual organizational strategies set and operationalized and aligned horizontally and vertically<br>Balanced scorecard in use | All team decisions are aligned with the strategy<br>Action plans and regular reviews used to execute strategic objectives<br>Strategic and operating decisions are systematically validated and adjusted<br>Periodic inspections to ensure that all organizational activities directly link to strategy | Business reviews used to link strategy to activities from top to bottom of the organization<br>Strategic plans engage thought diversity from broader organization<br>Market sensing is used to identify emerging opportunities, business strategy fit to market needs, barriers to execution | Execution of strategic objectives:<br>• Shared mindset metric<br>• Employee percent of time spent on strategic activities<br>• Employee rating of whether their suggestion are heard and acted upon |
| Leadership Accountability | Clear roles and accountabilities for each team member<br>Defined decision-making process | Roles executed and regularly reviewed and modified<br>Interdependent activities well-understood and actively managed<br>Members form teams to solve organizational problems without GM involvement | Members behave as leaders of the business, not just their unit<br>Members set agendas | Organizational alignment |
| Executive Collaboration | Team challenge is clear and challenging, but doable<br>Team rules of engagement defined<br>Meeting objectives and standard agendas set<br>Reality-based discussions about business issues and capabilities<br>Conflict management process clear | Rules of engagement engrained in team culture and member behaviors<br>Meetings focus on decisions and all decisions include follow-up<br>Open feedback and continuous improvement of team capabilities<br>Diverse perspectives and dialogues expose reality and produce new ideas<br>Members encourage horizontal linkages across boundaries | Members leverage teammates for problem solving<br>Open and honest dialogue about the team and its members<br>Members read each others' concerns<br>Members hold one another accountable for team behavior<br>Members walk the talk | Team commitment survey results |
| Leadership Growth | All key leaders assessed, prioritized, and known to top team<br>Assess organizational leaders with a single standard<br>Realistic, fact-based assessment | Best senior managers placed in appropriate positions; few failures<br>Year-over-year changes in leadership performance known | "Culture of leadership" emerges<br>Strategic management institutionalized | Pipeline metrics or substitute-to-star ratio<br>External reputation for leadership excellence<br>Employee engagement survey ratings on leadership question<br>High potential loss |

right (e.g., new compensation system, organizational redesign). Examples may include:

- Shift from a fixed- to variable-cost model
- A new outsourcing business
- A new solution set for a customer segment

Each strategic objective must include a measure of performance, someone on the executive team who agrees to accept ownership, a set of performance milestones, and a schedule of reviews for the next twelve months. The team leader should not be the assigned leader for any strategic objective. He/she is the owner of all objectives but is not the assigned leader of any one.

Once strategic objectives are set, executive team members brainstorm the four to six critical success factors—the internal capabilities the organization must get right to deliver its strategic objectives. These CSFs may not matter to customers but are barriers to the execution of the strategic objectives. Examples may include:

- More effective product development process
- Improved solution selling capabilities
- Stronger return on marketing investments
- Movement to a high-performance culture

Have executive team members brainstorm a long list of factors, then edit by matrixing CSFs with the strategic objectives (SOs), as shown in Table 4-2. This matrix will help team members judge whether their plan is sufficient to deliver the strategic objectives. Notice here that several CSFs have broad impact while others do not; also, some SOs are addressed by several CSFs while some are not.

**Model #3: Manage for Organizational Capability Growth.** A third option for focusing executive team performance is to balance short-term performance results with longer term capability improvements. The model presented in Table 4-3 may be a good fit for an executive

*Table 4-2. Finalizing critical success factors and strategic objectives.*

|  | SO #1 | SO #2 | SO #3 | SO #4 | CSF Metrics | CSF Owner |
|---|---|---|---|---|---|---|
| CSF #1 | ✓ | ✓ |  | ✓ |  |  |
| CSF #2 |  | ✓ |  |  |  |  |
| CSF #3 | ✓ |  |  | ✓ |  |  |
| CSF #4 | ✓ |  |  |  |  |  |
| CSF #5 |  | ✓ |  |  |  |  |
| CSF #6 |  | ✓ | ✓ |  |  |  |
| CSF #7 | ✓ | ✓ |  | ✓ |  |  |
| SO Metrics |  |  |  |  |  |  |
| SO Owner |  |  |  |  |  |  |

team with P&L accountability, where the team is required to meet both short-term financial, customer, and operational commitments and longer term capability improvements. The content of the table comes from the book *What Really Works* (HarperCollins, 2003) by William Joyce, Nitin Nohria, and Bruce Roberson, a project described as "the world's most systematic large-scale study of the practices that create business winners."

The project team was made up of sixteen professors from ten of the world's leading business schools and twenty-two McKinsey consultants. They studied the ten-year performance of 160 companies, sifting through more than 200 management practices to find the few that really mattered to business performance. The four primary practices are presented in Table 4-3.

*Table 4-3. A scorecard for assessing executive team performance.*

| EXECUTIVE TEAM RESULT | PHASE 1 | PHASE 2 | PHASE 3 |
|---|---|---|---|
| Strategy | Formalized strategy development process | Strategy development includes a variety of stakeholders | Strategic goal alignment from to bottom |
| | Broadly communicated strategies | All managers can state the strategic objectives and CSFs | Market sensing and feedback |
| Execution | Makes costs budget | Meets key customer, operational, and financial objectives most of the time | Reliably meets customer, operational, and financial quarterly objectives |
| | Business unit productivity plans set | All managers know unit productivity goal | Productivity improves to plan |
| Culture | Culture operationalized and accepted by employees | Systematic, measured approach for culture improvement set | Score improvements to plan on defined cultural dimensions |
| Structure | Plan to reduce unnecessary bureaucracy | Unrelenting fight against bureaucracy seen as cultural hallmark | Employees feel unnecessary bureaucracy is under control |

## How to Build a System for Effectively Measuring and Managing Key Results

The executive team, as a team, defines success and builds a system for ensuring that aspirations turn to results. The model presented here is a top-down one. Once executive team results have been defined, accountability for year-over-year performance on each team result must be assigned to one or more team members. This is not to say that the assigned member is solely accountable for performance improvements; rather, the member is accountable for leadership on this task; ownership is shared among all members.

A system for measuring and managing to team results requires rethinking the team scorecard to make sure that each result is prominently displayed. It also requires rethinking meetings so that you can state: (1) at which meeting each will be addressed, (2) who runs the meeting, and (3) what the standing agenda will be. Finally, an effective system requires a phased plan with milestones. When will the team reach Phase 2 on a particular team result? How will it be measured, and what specifically must be addressed to get from here to there?

## Conclusion

No organization can win until it has a differentiated strategy that adds value to customers and shareholders, and all members of the organization—from top to bottom—are precisely aligned to deliver that strategy. Getting the strategy right and effectively executed requires a high-performing executive team. This is the first required step for creating sustained competitive advantage through people.

The Human Capital Strategy addresses executive team performance through a top-down, results-based approach that answers the question "Is the performance of this executive team better than last year?" This chapter employs HCS principles to improve the performance of executive teams in order to affirmatively state that the performance of executive teams across the organization have improved year-over-year.

## Notes

1. S. Kaplan and B. Minton, "How has CEO Turnover Changed?" National Bureau of Economic Research, Working Paper 12465 (August 2006).

2. "Leadership IQ Study: Management, Inaction Among the Real Reasons Why CEOs Get Fired," PR Web Press Release Newswire, Washington, D.C. (June 15, 2005).

3. M. Buckingham and C. Coffman, First, Break all the Rules (New York: Simon & Schuster, 1999).

# Chapter Five

# Leaders Who Deliver Results

*"Are your leaders better than last year?"*

A fter a string of poor business reviews, a CEO becomes concerned about leadership capabilities and asks the CHRO to improve leadership performance. Here are two different approaches for handling the request. Which sounds like your organization?

*Scenario #1.* The CHRO presents the problem to her direct report team and asks for a plan from each department. The head of management development searches the leadership development literature and speaks to professional colleagues and consulting firms to identify state-of-the-art leadership development programs. She defines success as more courses, better attended, with improved satisfaction ratings. The talent manager has been getting good feedback from the annual succession plan and thinks, "Line executives like our process. This is not my problem," but he makes connections with a few top HR organizations to tighten up the process. The compensation leader looks at the performance ratings of all leaders and suggests terminating the bottom performers. The staffing leader says, "When you manage out the weak ones, I will be standing by to hire replacements."

*Scenario #2.* The CHRO asks the head of leadership (HL) to partner with a senior executive sponsor to build a comprehensive plan for improving year-over-year, leadership performance. The HL and the executive sponsor segment the company's top leaders into two segments—vice presidents and directors. They then facilitate a dialogue among the top team about how the team will define leadership performance for each segment. For vice presidents, performance is defined and measured by the following leadership results:

- Sets and executes strategies and plans that add significant customer or shareholder value.

- Improves organizational capability.

- Creates a challenging and fun work climate.

- Improves leadership performance of managers throughout the organization.

The HL then creates targeted developmental activities to improve performance of each leadership result. All developmental activities that are not aligned to one of the four results are mothballed. At the end of the year, the HL and executive sponsor report year-over-year changes in each leadership result by segment, as well as where changes occurred and why.

Notice the difference in the two approaches. Scenario #1 is program-centric, generated from the bottom up, with ownership that is fragmented by HR discipline. Scenario #2 is results-centric, generated from the top down, and owned by the line but led by an accountable HR leader. The underlying theory behind Scenario #2 is that HR is accountable for producing world-class leaders. Scenario #2 answers the question: "Are our leaders better than last year?"

## Leadership Development: The Current State

It is not difficult to convince executives of the importance of great leadership. A Conference Board study[1] of 400 CEOs found that by 2008, "developing and retaining potential leaders" will be second only to "retaining customers" as their company's most important business issue.[1] A 2005 study by RHR International provides partial insight on why this is so. The study found that 50 percent of companies surveyed believed that more than half of their senior leaders would leave within the next five years.[2]

Many executives are suspicious of leadership development programs that consume time and money and produce little change. Are these suspicions justified? Let's look at some data:

- The classic study *The War for Talent* (Harvard Business School Press, 2001), by Ed Michaels, Helen Handfield-Jones, and Beth Axelrod, found that only 7 percent of 6,900 managers surveyed believe their companies have sufficient leadership capabilities to pursue their most promising growth opportunities.

- A 2002 Corporate Leadership Council study of 19,000 employees in twenty-nine countries found that "people management training" improved productivity by only 2 percent.[3] Straight training approaches do not seem to deliver business results.

- A large, global Conference Board study in 2003 found that only 36 percent of companies rated their leadership capability to execute strategies as good or excellent, down from 50 percent a few years earlier.[4] Despite heavy investments in leadership development, the number of leaders who can execute strategies may be getting worse, not better.

- Accenture's 2004 High Performance Workforce Study found that while 65 percent of surveyed executives felt that developing effective leadership capabilities was very important, only 8 percent feel their company does a very good job at this.[5]

- Despite exponential growth in more sophisticated training programs and technologies, satisfaction with training is also getting worse. Accenture's 2006 High Performance Workforce Study found that the percent of executives who are very satisfied with their training function has fallen from a low 16 percent in 2004 to an even lower 10 percent in 2006.[6]

It's not that companies do not provide leadership training, succession planning, or talent assessment. Recent research indicates that the majority of companies use all three.[7] What's going on? It's simple: Companies are using development approaches aligned to today's HR model and misaligned with good human capital principles. The fix requires a shift to a new paradigm that is externally oriented and results-based.

## Leadership Performance

The important question to answer here is: *"Are your leaders better this than last year?"* The reason that so few managers can answer this question is that "better" is elusive. A clear, results-based definition of leadership, broadly accepted and stable over time, is the foundation for leadership performance improvements. Unfortunately, such definitions are rare. Few top teams have sat down to establish a common point of view around leadership. By default, management development trainers either implicitly or explicitly set the definition when they build leadership development courses. The result is lack of clarity around what it means to be a great leader and what to do to reach that ideal.

Companies with more sophisticated leadership development processes might say they have defined leadership through customized leadership competency models. If this sounds like your company, stop a manager in the hallway and ask, "What do great leaders do?" Does she recite the competency model? If so, can she remember the leadership competencies unassisted? If not, the leadership competency model is not driving daily behavior or value to customers, shareholders, or employees.

Few leadership competency models measure performance results; most measure personal characteristics and behaviors. Competencies are a means to an end; leadership results are the end. Here are a few misuses of competencies today.

**Misuse #1: The Design of Competencies.** Leadership competencies of even the most respected companies are often a mixed bag of skills (e.g., strategic thinking), personality traits (e.g., drive to achieve), knowledge (e.g., functional expertise), and talents (e.g., intelligence). This is a problem because knowledge and skills can be improved but personality traits and talents cannot.

In past corporate talent management roles, I often found it frustrating to assess the same executives year-after-year with a corporate leadership competency model that went, "He still does not have sufficient drive to achieve. Tell him and get him more development." Drive to achieve is largely innate or developed at a young age. It is very unlikely that a mature adult can be trained to be a high achiever. Reassessing leaders each year on their drive to achieve is like a basketball coach saying, "You are still too short, and we all know height is important. Work on it and come back next year." As Peter Drucker said:

> How one performs is unique. It is a matter of personality. Whether personality be a matter of nature or nurture, it is surely formed long before a person goes to work. . . . A person's way of performing can be slightly modified, but is unlikely to be completely changed—and certainly not easily.[8]

Dean Walsh of Sullivan-Walsh Consulting put it this way: "It is impractical and often impossible to change *who a person is*. It is far more practical to tell a person *what to do*."[9] Mr. Walsh uses the metaphor of a children's basketball league. One coach yells at the children to play more aggressively. Another coach tells them, "I want your shoulder to be no more than twelve inches from your opponent's shoulder the whole game." Whose team will be more likely to improve? If you want to improve leadership performance, help leaders understand what to do, not whom to be.

**Misuse #2: Substituting Less Valid Predictors for More Valid Predictors.** Several years ago, I met with an executive, George, who had been turned down for a promotion to a senior sales role with as the Managing Director of a large global account. The role was similar to the one he currently held, but with a larger account. George had more than a decade of experience at the company and had turned around some of its toughest accounts. The reason he was not promoted was because, in a competency-based structured interview conducted by a consultant from a well-known firm, George had failed to talk about his relationship management experiences. This generated a score of zero on the relationship management competency and caused him to fail the interview.

Two of the corporation's senior-most executives vouched for George's relationship management capabilities. They said they had watched George work for more than a decade and were confident that relationship management was a strength. However, the consulting firm insisted that their assessment tool was valid and convinced the CHRO to turn George down. George left the company soon after.

The maxim "Past behavior is the best predictor of future behavior" is to the field of psychology what "supply and demand" is to economics. When a person's next role is similar to a current or past role, as in George's case, but perhaps larger in scope, past performance is the best predictor of future performance. Think about it. Which is a better predictor of future performance of a World Cup player—past goals and assists, or the results from a competency-based interview? In George's case, a results-based assessment of relationship management might have reviewed past data to answer the question "How have relationships between George's clients and our company changed throughout his tenure?" A results-based assessment would likely have resulted in a promotion.

## WHAT IS VALIDITY?

Validity does not mean that an assessment tool will make a correct prediction. It only means that using the tool to assess a large number of candidates will predict the best candidate more effectively than a coin flip. A coin flip assessment will choose the best candidate 50 percent of the time (this is an average over a large number of candidates). Without going into statistical detail, if an assessment tool reliably increases the hit rate to 55 percent, it may be a statistically valid predictor. Validity does not mean the tool is the best predictor, nor does validity imply that the difference is meaningful. An incremental increase of 5 percentage points may be statistically significant and render the tool "valid," but it might not produce a meaningful improvement.

The important point here is not that competencies or assessment tools are bad. It is that even the best assessment tools include error. The practical challenge is to find and use tools with the most predictive power and the least error. When past behavior is available and the new task is similar, past performance will be your best assessment tool. Don't trade A-level predictors for B-level predictors. And don't accept the consulting firm argument that because their tool is "valid," it provides accurate and meaningful predictions.

**Misuse #3: Mixing Competencies into Performance Appraisals.** Let's say that you are a regional manager with P&L responsibility. You have contracted with your boss to: (1) deliver a specified profit amount, (2) exceed a threshold on customer satisfaction, and (3) fill the sales pipeline with a specified number of new projects for the following year. At the end of the year, you have exceeded your plan on all three measures. However, your boss gives you an average rating, stating that you are low on your "attention to detail" competency. How would you feel?

Appraisals are a contract between you and your boss. They measure results on commitments; either you achieved the commitment or you did not. If you made your plan but received a low score on "attention to detail," then one or more of the following may have been true:

- Attention to detail was incorrectly assessed.

- Attention to detail was not a differentiator for regional manager excellence.

- You had towering strengths that overcame your weakness on detail.

- You kept a detail person on your team to compensate for your weakness.

Does focusing exclusively on results violate the principle of a balanced approach (i.e., the what and how) to leadership? At General Electric, "what" and "how" ratings are used, but they are not confused with leadership competencies. The "how" at GE was designed to align behaviors with corporate values such as boundarylessness and intolerance of bureaucracy. GE's "how" makes it clear that the company wants results, but those results must be achieved in ways that strengthen the desired corporate culture. Competencies are not the "how"; they are the "what." Unless competence in "attention to detail" is a corporate value, it should not be used to appraise performance.

**Misuse #4: Using Competencies for Leadership Assessment.** More and more companies are beginning to conduct annual talent assessments to determine leadership performance and potential. Consulting firms that sell talent assessments often define great leadership by 360° feedback results on their proprietary survey tools. These assessments make competencies primary and results secondary. This begs the question: "Should leadership excellence be defined by competencies or by sustained business results?" Peter Drucker said, "Effective leadership is not about making speeches or being liked; leadership is defined by results, not attributes."[10] Whether or not Winston Churchill was a pacesetter should be irrelevant to an assessment of his leadership performance.

The first problem with using competencies to assess leadership performance is that competency models have an underlying assumption that all leaders must possess all competencies—the assumption of the "Renaissance Leader." As Drucker said: ". . . we are not going to breed a new race of supermen. We will have to run our organizations with men as they are." He goes on to say: "What seems to be wanted is universal genius, and universal genius has always been in short supply . . . we cannot expect to get the executive performance we need by raising our standards for abilities, let alone by hoping for the universally gifted man."[11]

An important purpose of an organization is to pull people with complementary skills together so that the organization can do something that no one person can do alone. The leadership team, rather than any individual member, must possess all the competencies. For example, if you are great at vision and strategy but poor at detail, you have two options: (1) become good at detail, or (2) hire a person who is good at detail.

The second problem with using competencies to assess leadership performance is related to the first: Competency models focus on weaknesses. We will see in Chapter 7 that performance management systems that emphasize performance and personality weaknesses reduce performance. Author and consultant Marcus Buckingham has done a great service to organizations by presenting solid data that shows the benefits of focusing on strengths rather than on weaknesses. Buckingham's research concludes: "Great managers would offer you this advice: Focus on a person's strengths and manage around his weaknesses. Don't try to fix weaknesses. Don't try to perfect each person . . . help each person become more of who he already is."[12]

The third problem is the confusion between what a person is capable of doing versus what he/she actually does. Earlier in my career, I became acquainted with a very smart, dapper general manager from Australia. Let's call him Joe. Joe looked great. He had a shiny shaved head and wore beautiful suits. His interpersonal style was engaging and very intelligent. Joe was impressive. Joe often visited headquarters, where he made the rounds, charming the staff and dazzling them with his ideas. Year after year, Joe received the highest possible rating in "strategic thinking." However, when we looked into the data for the past four years, we found that Joe's profits, share, and revenue had dropped each year. In addition, we were never able to identify a strategy that Joe had actually set and executed. In the end, whether or not Joe is a strategic thinker is irrelevant to shareholders. They care only that Joe create and execute strategies. Maybe he can do that with his own intellectual capabilities or maybe he does it through including that capability on his leadership team. Results, not individual competencies, are important to business success.

## Building Leadership Excellence: A Roadmap

Creating leadership excellence requires a blueprint of success and a fully integrated system for delivering that vision. Success is not world-class leadership development but best-in-industry leaders. What results define best-in-industry leaders, and what do these leaders do to deliver those results? This section presents the roadmap (shown in Figure 5-1) for building a system that improves year-over-year leadership perform-

*Figure 5-1. The Human Capital Management model.*

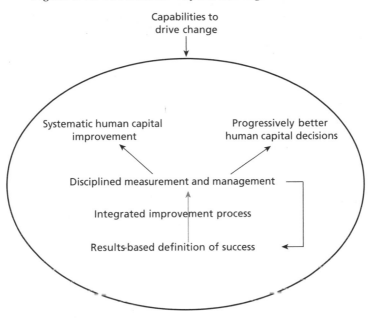

ance results. The first step is to create organizational capabilities and accountabilities sufficient for growing leaders.

## Organizational Capabilities for Improving Leadership Performance

Who is accountable for improving leadership performance in your organization? For most companies, many departments have a role, but nobody is accountable designing and executing an integrated plan. The first step in improving the performance of leaders is to build sufficient organizational capabilities to grow this important asset.

Years ago, consumer product organizations encountered a similar dilemma: Who would be accountable for the growth of products? R&D was in charge of the design, manufacturing produced it, and sales sold it, but there was no clear accountability for the actual product or brand performance. The result was a management innovation—brand management. A brand manager's role is clear: They must grow brand profits. They do not own manufacturing or sales, but they must influence these functions to succeed. Brand managers typically create and deploy marketing programs throughout the year. They are happy when they win advertising awards, but they know they will lose their jobs if they do not produce business value in the form of profits. Brand managers use programs as a means to an end.

The brand management archetype works well for improving leadership performance. It begins with a brand manager or brand management team who is accountable for year-over-year performance improvements for a defined set of leaders. This person or team may not own all the required parts but must influence and remain accountable for improvements in leadership. Programs are simply a means—in many cases, an important means—to that end. Shifting from today's program-centric model of leadership development to a results-based, brand management model will accelerate leadership growth and performance. A method for creating and executing a brand management approach to leadership growth follows.

**Segment Leadership Roles.** A primary task of every Chief Marketing Officer is to segment by customer set to determine the target market. Each customer set has different needs, and members of the customer set buy products that help them meet those demands. The same is true with leadership. Different leadership roles require unique types of support and development that help incumbents meet the demands of the business. One-size-fits-all leadership competencies are similar to one-size-fits-all marketing approaches—not optimally effective.

There are several ways to segment your leaders (as shown in Figure 5-2). One way is to segment by organizational levels—executives, middle managers, and supervisors. The results for executive leaders are often different from those for middle managers, which are in turn different from those for supervisors.

Another way of segmenting is by critical leadership roles (e.g., sales managers, store managers, R&D managers). In many cases, segmenting and managing by leadership role sharpens focus, and as with almost any activity, the sharper the focus, the more efficient the change. Segmenting by roles enables a company to move from generic to very specific leadership results.

*Figure 5-2. Methods of segmenting and managing leaders.*

**Build the Brand Management Infrastructure.** There are several ways to create a brand management infrastructure. The first is to assign an executive or a small executive team to own a target segment. For example, one executive team might "brand manage" the region managers. Success might be assessed by measurable year-over-year leadership performance improvements as well as the quality and quantity of candidates in the regional manager pipeline.

A second way to assign ownership is to create a small, full-time team of top segment performers to be accountable for leadership development. (See Figure 5-3.) For example, if a company has 1,000 retail units, a team of two to three of the highest performing and most innovative retail unit managers can work together full-time for a defined period of time to improve the performance of the retail unit managers.

*Figure 5-3. Leadership development governance model.*

This retail manager leadership team becomes accountable for year-over-year performance improvements of the 1,000 unit managers even though the retail managers remain formally aligned to their district manager. The leadership team formally reports to a board of directors consisting of the highest performing and most creative district managers. This governance structure requires a larger investment than the first method, but in my experience, it produces outstanding results. Chapter 6 will provide additional detail on the governance structure. Think about it. What is the incremental value to customers and shareholders of a 5 percent performance improvement of 1,000 unit managers? If you don't know, you need a Human Capital Management system.

## A Results-Based Definition of Leadership

Perhaps by now we can agree that great leadership should be defined by sustained business results rather than by competencies. Competencies are more appropriately used for diagnosing why leadership performance is low (or high), for creating developmental activities, and for predicting performance in new and different roles.

If you choose to go with the one-size-fits-all leadership model, consider the four leadership results below. Notice that all four dimensions are results that matter to customers and shareholders. Each must be assigned one or more measures of success:

1. Set and execute a plan that adds significant value to customers and shareholders.

2. Improve organizational capabilities; the organization must become more capable of delivering business value every year.

3. Reliably deliver short-term commitments.

4. Improve the skills and performance of people in the organization.

Alternatively, you may choose to segment by leadership role. The cost is complexity; the benefit is a more focused and concrete set of leadership results. Table 5-1 presents a results-based profile for a real estate office manager. For a real estate company, the answer to the question

*Table 5-1. Sample leadership results for a real estate office manager.*

| LEADERSHIP RESULT | MEASURES |
|---|---|
| Maintain best in area agents | **Lagging**<br>Percent of agents on the top 100 list in the county<br><br>**Leading**<br>Employee satisfaction survey<br>Percent of top agents hired in calendar year |
| Fully networked in community | **Lagging**<br>Percent of real estate managers and/or developers in the local area with whom you meet at least twice a year<br><br>**Leading**<br>Active membership in community organizations<br>Articles/interviews in local publications |
| Grow future agents | **Lagging**<br>Percent of new hires at $1M after 12 months<br><br>**Leading**<br>Address book of those on prospective client lists<br>Agent relationships |
| Brand awareness | **Lagging**<br>Local market research study on quality of real estate firms<br><br>**Leading**<br>Advertising quantity and quality / $ spent |

"Are your leaders better this year than last year?" is determined by yearly changes on the four leadership results across all of the company's real estate office managers, as shown in the table.

Let's look at another example, this time for sales managers in Table 5-2. The three key results shown are leading indicators—the most important results a sales manager must deliver to drive revenue growth and customer satisfaction improvements. The model tells sales managers which activities are most important for delivering each key result and the performance measures that will be used to monitor progress on each key result. In addition, the model helps company executives know how sales managers' performance has changed year-over-year and why.

*Table 5-2. Key results for sales managers.*

| KEY RESULT | ACTIVITIES | PERFORMANCE MEASURES |
|---|---|---|
| Match sales reps to accounts | Understand opportunities by account<br>Find good chemistry between rep personality/talent and client<br>Balance workload among reps<br>Reassign reps to maximize growth | Client satisfaction with sales reps<br>Sales productivity (sales/rep)<br>Rep satisfaction with assignment |
| Track and forecast revenue | Align account plan with pipeline<br>Use pipeline to manage daily activities<br>Provide coaching and support during pipeline reviews | Sales forecasts are accurate<br>Pipeline revenue equals $3 \times$ quota |
| Manage sales and service escalations | Define when escalations are appropriate<br>Determine appropriate escalation information<br>Instruct reps to sell interval terms that reduce escalations | Number of escalations<br>Company hours spent on escalations<br>Provisioning department satisfaction with manager escalations |

Although it would be unusual if a given sales manager consistently delivers revenue and customer satisfaction without performing well on the key results, that would be fine. Key results are a means to an end, and that end is about consistently producing results that matter to customers and shareholders.

## Creating Integrated Leadership Development Initiatives

The important question to ask here is: *Are your leadership development efforts necessary and sufficient to improve leadership performance?* Once ownership and accountability for leadership performance is assigned and successful leadership is defined, the next step is to create an integrated and systemic approach to leadership development.

There are three ways organizations can improve business performance through leadership. The first is short-term: improving in-year leadership performance results. The second is mid-term: filling the pipeline with qualified candidates for promotion or movement. The third is long-term: growing high potentials. The most critical condition for achieving these objectives is to create a leadership culture, so let's start there.

**Building a Leadership Culture.** I joined IBM in Tokyo in late 2001 and was invited to visit a high-potential assessment center that my new team was running in a hotel outside the city. Attending were twelve young, non-executive high potentials who went through a battery of assessments for three long days and nights. I was very surprised to learn that the six assessors were the senior-most executives of IBM Asia-Pacific. They included the general manager of IBM Australia–New Zealand, two of the six Asia-Pacific industry GMs, and the Asia-Pacific CFO. IBM is a company that manages quarter-to-quarter—all nonessential activity shuts down about three weeks before the quarter ends. This was not only two weeks before the end of a quarter, but midway through the last month of the fiscal year; and six of IBM Asia-Pacific's most critical executives were locked up for three days and nights with twelve young high potentials. That is a leadership culture, and *that* is why IBM has some of the world's finest leaders.

Best practice teams often come to IBM to benchmark the company's executive development workshops and talent management process. These teams are missing the point. IBM's talent management systems are indeed solid and provide a necessary foundation for leadership growth, but that is not why IBM has outstanding leaders. The reason is culture.

Plenty of research supports the assertion that a leadership culture is the key. A 2003 Corporate Leadership Council study examined 276 organizations and statistically sorted through 195 methods for improving leadership performance. They then ranked the 195 methods from most to least effective at producing real leadership performance change.[13]

Here are the most important drivers in order of impact (culture-related drivers are italicized):

- *Senior executives are good role models for developing employees.*
- *Executives believe development is important.*

- The organization modifies development based on organizational strategy.
- *Line managers make development a priority.*
- The organization allows candidate's future direct reports to influence hiring.
- *The organization publicly recognizes managers for developing employees.*
- External candidates are compatible with other executives.
- *Managers are held accountable for development in performance reviews.*

When it comes to leadership excellence, data suggests that the most important thing to get right is culture. *Chief Executive Magazine* and Hewitt Associates' annual Top Companies for Leaders project identified a similar relationship between companies with high-performing leaders and a leadership culture. Their data indicated that the average CEO spends 10 percent of his/her time developing leaders while those in the top companies are spending more than 25 percent of their time developing leaders. Their data also indicated that when a CEO is actively involved in leadership development, the organization averages a 22 percent return to shareholders over a three-year period, as opposed to a *negative* 4 percent return for companies where the CEO is not directly involved.[14]

Fortunately, many executives see the importance of spending their time growing leaders and believe they can do better. A 2006 McKinsey report found that although senior executives see effective talent management as an important strategic priority, they feel they are underperforming.[15] These executives do not blame talent management processes even when they say the processes can be improved. Rather, they blame themselves and their business managers for failing to devote sufficient time and attention to talent management and development.

**Improving In-Year Leadership Performance.** In-year leadership performance improvements require a laser-like focus on a few clearly defined leadership results. Many companies boast about their large training catalogue of classroom and e-learning leadership courses. That is a program-centric, bottoms-up approach. The New Human Capital Strategy uses a more focused approach. All developmental efforts must explicitly align to one or more of the leadership results or be eliminated.

The best developmental plans use a variety of learning methods. In my experience, the most effective developmental tools for improving short-term performance are business reviews, quality coaching, and action learning. Of these three, consistent and disciplined business reviews may be the best tool of all.

- *Business Reviews.* I was asked once to create general management training for a large Japanese organization that had just reorganized into industry segments, each with P&L accountabilities. Prior to the change, sales executives had been in charge of revenue and customer satisfaction, but not for profit. As I began the task of thinking through a general management curriculum, a senior executive told me, "No training is necessary. Every time Mr. Tanaka comes in, I will ask about outstanding receivables. I assure you, he will get the message." Our solution was not a two-week mini-MBA class. General manager development was achieved by a balanced scorecard, and an effective business review. The point here is not to assume that training is the most effective lever for developing leaders.

- *Coaching.* After business reviews, the next most important activity for improving short-term leadership performance is coaching. Coaching sessions tied to business reviews are just-in-time and highly job relevant.

- *Action Learning.* The third most effective developmental activity is action learning. Action learning is real work that also improves employees' skills. I am a strong advocate of action learning and feel that almost all training should produce tangible and immediate benefit to the company. For example, traditional sales pipeline management training might change to a workshop where sales leaders bring in data and fill the pipeline. Contrast this to the many generic management education or leadership courses offered today.

**Filling the Leadership Pipeline.** The leadership pipeline is becoming a very hot topic given the impending retirement of the first wave of baby boomers. Consequently, talent management, one of the newest HR professions, is getting a lot of attention. Many companies today have talent management systems, but few CEOs seem comfortable with their current leadership pipelines.

With so many companies having succession planning systems, why then are so many executives concerned about their leadership pipelines? Because process and programs are, too often, the focus of talent management rather than real results. Leadership pipeline improvements require not only succession planning but systematic leadership growth, and that requires a system, not a collection of great programs. Talent management professionals are not accountable for leadership growth. They are accountable for a well-performing succession planning process. Look at how your talent management staff spends its time. Is it in meetings to improve the succession process/technologies, or is it on projects aligned with the blueprint for leadership excellence?

In the 2003 Corporate Leadership Council study discussed earlier that ranked the impact of 195 drivers of leadership quality, 45 of the 195 drivers were talent management practices (e.g., 360 reviews, talent review meetings, assessment centers, behavioral interviews, succession for all above a certain level, manager's willingness to give up talent, tell/don't tell high potentials of their status).[17] The result? Not a single talent management practice ended up in the top 34 practices associated with leadership quality—not one.

So what does it all mean? It does *not* mean that talent management processes and practices should be discarded. It simply means that processes, by themselves, do not significantly impact leadership performance. Continuing to tighten up talent management processes will not deliver improvements in leadership performance or pipeline. You must set the blueprint and build a system for delivering the blueprint.

Long-term leadership improvements require an integrated, systemic approach. The succession plan must be connected with the placement process, which must be connected to development, appraisals, and business reviews. Success requires an integrated system, not world-class programs. Here is a simple roadmap for building a system that strengthens the leadership pipeline.

- *Define pipeline success.* This begins by identifying the most important leadership segments and defining pipeline success by segment. For example, "We will increase the number of sales managers fully qualified for promotion to sales center vice president from twenty-five to thirty-five by [date]."

- *Conduct results-based assessments of all leaders by segment.* Once leadership results have been operationalized and measures set by target leadership segment, all leaders must be assessed. Perceived fairness is critical. A leadership assessment process that is perceived as subjective and politically biased will quickly destroy a performance culture. Assessment criteria should be results-based and objectively measurable.

- *Use talent pools.* Many succession management strategies are annually set plans that quickly become obsolete as people and roles change. Consider using talent pools in addition to, or in place of, replacement benches. Quite simply, a talent pool is a pool of leaders with similar skills. For example, if we have ten good marketing managers and we need thirty-two given the company's growth objectives, we might need a pool of fifty potential marketing managers from which we will carefully monitor developmental progress.

- *Focus and motivate those in leadership pipelines.* Make sure that all those in the talent pool understand what they must demonstrate to be promoted. Tell them where they are now vis à vis those requirements and the specific results they must deliver to demonstrate that they are ready for promotion. Set the bar with clear performance measures, and let managers decide if they want to try to jump it.

- *Use succession information to make thoughtful placement decisions.* Leadership development research consistently shows that the most effective development is experiential. If you want an athlete to become a great swimmer, make sure she swims everyday. If you want a leader to be a strategic thinker, assign her to the strategy group to think strategically everyday.

*Table 5-3. The five-minute drill.*

Unannounced Changes

| NAME | FROM | TO |
| --- | --- | --- |
| Terry Jones | Sales Director, London | Regional VP, Paris |

Open Positions

| POSITION/INCUMBENT/BAND | POSITION DESCRIPTION | CANDIDATE SLATE/BAND |
| --- | --- | --- |
| GM, Manufacturing—Singapore/Andy Puah/(C) | Leads six plants in the ASEAN region | Tae Yeong Lee (C)<br>Chris Wong (D)<br>Eric Chang (D) |

People to be Moved

| POSITION/INCUMBENT/BAND | POSITION DESCRIPTION | CANDIDATE SLATE/BAND |
| --- | --- | --- |
| Kathy Green | Sales VP, Auckland | Regional marketing or customer support |

IBM is particularly effective in executive placement. The company uses a simple process to make placement decisions called a five-minute drill (see Table 5-3).[18] The five-minute drill, which actually takes thirty minutes or more, is the first scheduled item on the monthly top team meeting for each IBM business unit. There are three topics discussed: (1) executive position changes since last month, (2) open positions and candidate slates, and (3) people to be moved. The attendees discuss and debate candidate slates, but the final decision rests with the hiring manager.

• *Create ongoing leadership development dialogue.* Annual succession planning reviews are rarely sufficient to produce real changes in the leadership pipeline. For organizations that have a cadence of annual reviews, consider supplementing annual reviews with quarterly updates for assessing talent readiness by leadership pool. Let's say that the sales manager pool is a target population for discussion. Sales executives from various business units would attend to discuss those in the pool, to decide whether developmental activities for each are sufficient to meet the defined pipeline objectives, to work through the politics of sharing talent, and so on.

## Growing High Potentials

In 2002, Grace Lee, the China general manager of a European company, was concerned that the business was growing faster than the capabilities of her leaders. Grace decided that the China subsidiary needed to accelerate the growth of its high potentials. To meet this challenge, Grace created the China 100, shorthand for China's top 100 high potentials. Each of the high potentials chose one of five critical roles: sales, project management, IT architecture, consulting, and general management. Success was defined as growing technical and leadership capabilities of the high-potential population faster than revenue. Grace's success with the challenge facing her was due to:

- An organization accountable for improvements in leadership growth
- A prescriptive roadmap with objective performance measures
- A strong cultural norm that leadership growth was important

Here is a roadmap to consider when growing your high potentials.

**Choosing Those with the Highest Potential.** This is the right time to use competencies rather than results. In many cases, results in entry-level roles are poor predictors of success in supervisory or middle management roles. For example, many entry-level consultants schedule team meetings and analyze spreadsheet data. The talent required for this detail work might be very different from the conceptual and influence skills required in more senior roles. In a review of recent research, the following competencies seem promising for predicting long-term potential:

- Influence and collaboration
- Drive to achieve/passion for winning
- Team leadership
- Integrity
- Flexible and adaptable

- Learning agility and speed
- Emotional intelligence
- Love of challenge

For the most part, you cannot build these competencies; you buy them. Thus, a smart purchase decision at the front end is critical. If there is no single accurate assessment tool—and there likely is not—use several assessment tools and triangulate. Just remember that tools assist you in your decision making; they are not designed to make the decisions for you.

Consider assessing all of the competencies in the list above (and any others you think important) to assess high potentials when beginning to deploy a Human Capital Management strategy. You may choose to use the results of only three to five of the competencies when making the actual decision, but by rating each competency and storing them in a Human Capital Management database, you will be able to statistically determine, over time, the most important competencies. Figure 5-4 presents another example of using regression to determine which competencies are most important. Take a look at performance ratings for each of the high potentials' first three years. In the example shown in Figure 5-4, love of a challenge is the most important predictor of performance, followed by drive to achieve/passion for winning.

**Assigning High Potentials to the Best Managers.** When I was a graduate student, my adviser, Jeff Sulzer, ran assessments of the graduates from the New Orleans Police Academy. Each year, there was a negative correlation between the academy assessment score and the first-year performance ratings, as experienced officers wanted to humble those with high test scores. Dr. Sulzer called this the "Smart Ass Effect." This effect went away over time, and the academy assessment proved to be a good predictor of long-term performance. It is important that new high potentials are assigned to the very best managers rather than to those who feel the need to put the new "smart asses" in their place. Putting your best people with poor managers quickly stunts development, creates dissatisfaction, and increases turnover.

*Figure 5-4. Identifying the most predictive*
*competencies of future performance.*

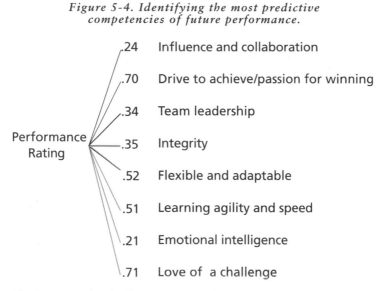

| | |
|---|---|
| .24 | Influence and collaboration |
| .70 | Drive to achieve/passion for winning |
| .34 | Team leadership |
| Performance Rating — .35 | Integrity |
| .52 | Flexible and adaptable |
| .51 | Learning agility and speed |
| .21 | Emotional intelligence |
| .71 | Love of a challenge |

*Note:* The data contained in this illustration is not real. It is for illustrative purposes only.

**Creating a Clear, Results-Based, Developmental Roadmap.** As with the China 100 example discussed earlier, consider breaking high potentials into professions, then create prescriptive, results-based developmental plans. High-potential employees have high needs for achievement. They want to know where they are, where they need to go, and how to get there.

Not only should every company be able to answer the question, "Are our high potentials better this year than last?" but every high potential should also know if he/she is a better leader this year than last. Just as no company would make financial investments without checking the return, no company should make time and money investments on high potentials without a clear understanding of the return.

**Assessing and Providing Feedback.** When he was at Allied Signal, Larry Bossidy insisted on annual assessments of a target group of high potentials. The assessments included having HR professionals interview fifteen to twenty high potential's direct reports, peers, subordinates, bosses, and customers. Executives said the practice changed company culture. "It legitimized development," commented one. "Now it's okay to have development needs and work on them."[19]

**Managing Key Developmental Experiences with Discipline.** As human beings, we grow through adversity and diversity. That is, we grow through difficult experiences that place us in new and different situations. Organizational psychology research is clear: The best way to develop leaders over the long term is to put them into new and challenging assignments. Morgan McCall of the University of Southern California's Marshall School has documented seven key development experiences for growing leaders:

1. Early work experiences
2. First supervision assignment
3. Start from scratch
4. Fix it/turnaround
5. Project/task force
6. Scope increase (e.g. people, budget, functions)
7. Line to staff/staff to line[20]

A Human Capital Management system must answer questions such as "Has the average number of key developmental experiences of those still in the program changed year-over-year?" "Which developmental experiences are we missing?" "Which populations are missing them?"

## Measuring and Managing with Discipline

It's December and the top team of your business unit wants a year-end summary of the unit's people. What do you present? You could present the number of classroom training days, turnover changes from the prior year, or performance rating distributions. Here is another idea: What if you presented an eight-slide PowerPoint presentation that looked like this:

*Leadership Performance*

1. Here are the four critical leadership roles we discussed at the beginning of the year.

2.  Here is what a 1-percent improvement in leadership performance is worth to revenue and profit for each of the four roles.

3.  Here is the change in average leadership performance in each segment for the last three years and the predicted impact on revenue.

4.  Here is what we learned last year about improving leadership performance *(with bullet-pointed lessons learned)*.

5.  Here are the coming year's investments for performance improvements and how we will assess performance changes.

## Leadership Pipeline

6.  Here are the most important leadership roles for delivering the business strategy and the number required by role over the next twelve months.

7.  Here are the criteria for promotion by leadership pool and the number qualified now and in six and twelve months to fill open positions.

8.  Here is the list of high potentials and changes in leadership results versus plan.

This is what it means to measure and manage human capital like financial capital. This is about results, not programs.

Marshall Goldsmith, a leading authority on leadership, wrote that he had been in the leadership development business for twelve years before one anyone asked him if it worked. His honest, yet embarrassed, reply was, "I don't know." Goldsmith wrote, "Historically, there has been little research to indicate that leadership development has made a positive, long-term difference. There has been almost no documentation that leaders changed or that organizations became more effective."[21]

When designing a global talent management process at a large European financial institution, I visited the European headquarters of one of the world's largest talent management and HR consulting firms. This firm had conducted thousands of executive assessments at my client organization each year for the previous three years. And each year, the consulting firm followed the assessments with a mandatory leadership training course for each person assessed.

I asked the woman at the consulting firm who was in charge of client data for its European region to send us the past three years of our assessment data because we wanted to review it for changes by executive to see how the assessments and training had changed behavior. She was intrigued. She said that this was her first request to analyze leadership changes over time by person. She said she had also wondered how the assessments and training worked and asked me to let her know what we learned.

It is difficult to imagine other large corporate investments with such undisciplined measures of return. Why are leadership investments held to a lower standard? Because many believe that human issues cannot be measured. This is not true; behavioral scientists* measure behavior of insects, animals, and people everyday. Measuring human behavior is quite possible.

## Measuring and Managing for Leadership Performance Improvements

The foundation for a disciplined human capital system is results-based measures of success. The more focused and clearly defined the measures, the better. The next step is to systematically capture the data in a way that accurately represents the leader's performance. This data must be stored in a database with other performance results, assessments, etc., to understand relationships over time.

The example shown in Table 5-4 is a long spreadsheet row cut into three pieces to fit on the page. (In a regular spreadsheet, these three would go side by side and extend off the page to the right.) Think about how such a database could be used to measure the performance of your managers. The columns from "Name" to "Manager ID" are demographics, or "independent variables," to sort the data. The columns to the right are measures of leadership performance, or "dependent variables."

---

*What's the difference between a behavioral scientist and a psychologist? Nothing. Behavioral science just sounds more legitimate.

*Table 5-4. An example of a leadership database.*

| NAME | PERFORMANCE RATING | | | TIME IN POSITION | FUNCTION | LOCATION | MANAGER ID | STRATEGY & EXECUTION | |
|---|---|---|---|---|---|---|---|---|---|
| | 0 3 | 0 4 | 0 5 | | | | | Manager Rating | Measure |
| Aki Tanaka | | | | | | | | | |

| NAME | ORGANIZATION CAPABILITY | | | SHORT-TERM COMMIT-MENTS | DEVELOP PEOPLE AND LEADERS | COMPETENCIES | | | | | |
|---|---|---|---|---|---|---|---|---|---|---|---|
| | Measure 1 | Measure 2 | Measure 3 | Measure | Measure | 1 | 2 | 3 | 1 | 2 | 3 |
| Aki Tanaka | | | | | | | | | | | |

| NAME | CLASSES/WORKSHOPS ATTENDED | | | OPERATIONAL RESULTS | | | | CUSTOMER RESULTS | | | FINANCIAL RESULTS | | |
|---|---|---|---|---|---|---|---|---|---|---|---|---|---|
| | Class 1 | Class 2 | Class 3 | Cert 1 | Cert 2 | Cert 3 | Cert 4 | 1 | 2 | 3 | 1 | 2 | 3 |
| Aki Tanaka | | | | | | | | | | | | | |

So, what will such a database tell us? It will tell us:

- Which managers and countries produce the best and worst leaders.

- How performance ratings are related to operational, customer, and financial (i.e., business) results.

- How competencies are related to appraisal ratings, leadership results, or business results.

- Which leadership results are most predictive of business results.

- Which competencies are better predictors than leadership results.

- Which units are growing their leaders fastest.

- Which competencies never improve, and which are malleable.

- The relationship between the developmental activities and success, and which activities are and are not producing a return on investment.

- How long it takes for a leader in a new role to hit peak performance.

- The ideal time in position.

- How long after beginning the role the performance of leaders begins to fall.

- How much revenue is lost transitioning to a new leader.

- Which units are sending their people to developmental activities, and which are not.

- Which leadership results are the best predictors of operational, customer, and financial results.

We can go on and on. Adding additional independent variables such as gender, high-potential status, and time in company and dependent variables such as employee engagement scores, employee voluntary and involuntary turnover, and key developmental experiences will provide even more insight.

A human capital database enables an organization to make better human capital decisions as it learns through experience. How difficult is it to create this database? It's easy. Which of the data do you have today? You probably have all of it; it just exists in different databases. You know the revenue growth, profit, customer satisfaction, and operational results by country, right? You know who has attended which training courses. You have 360° data. You have all the data, but you may not be using it. The task is simply to assemble and analyze the data you have on hand.

Consider creating a quarterly or biannual leadership report, broadly distributed, to strengthen the leadership culture by managing human capital with the discipline a company expects in managing its financial capital. In program-based approaches to leadership development, annual reports are a summary of programs, attendees, and course satisfaction ratings. But this is about results, not programs.

## Measuring and Managing Leadership Pipelines

Every company has multiple leadership pipelines. Each is tied to a defined leadership segment and is owned by an individual or team that manages the segment. Once leadership databases are created by segment (and rolled up into a common database), measuring and managing the pipeline becomes straightforward.

A pool of high potentials is defined for each segment and criteria is set for qualifications for promotion. For country managers, that may be: (1) success in at least one role with P&L, (2) high ratings on each of the four key leadership results, and (3) strong business performance for the past three years. Whatever algorithm is chosen, pipelines can be monitored and developmental experiences focused by using the leadership database.

## Conclusion

Great leaders are a potential source of sustained competitive advantage available to virtually all businesses. However, despite large investments in leadership development, many surveys today indicate a concern among business leaders about the capabilities of their leaders to fully execute today's and tomorrow's business plans. Why is today's approach not producing a sufficient volume of leaders? Because today's approach is more focused on building world-class leadership development programs than world-class leaders.

A top-down approach to leadership growth begins with a measurable, results-based definition of leadership success. The definition is based on the assumption that businesses exist to deliver economic returns to their owners, and as such, the true measure of leadership performance is sustained business results. This is a very different perspective from many of today's competency-based approaches that define success as competency assessment results. This results-based human capital approach makes leadership performance primary and views competencies as enablers of those results.

Once leadership success is operationalized, all developmental processes must be realigned to focus on growing one or more of the defined leadership results. Some of the most effective developmental tools for improving short-term performance are business reviews, coaching, and action learning.

Finally, a systematic approach to leadership performance improvements requires a disciplined measurement and management of leadership performance. Most companies have most, if not all, the data to measure leadership with discipline, but few use the data. Using objective data to grow leaders has several benefits: (1) success is operationalized and development is focused, (2) leaders and their managers become accountable for leadership performance improvements, and (3) the organization is able learn from its experience to make progressively better human capital decisions.

## Notes

1. Conference Board, "The CEO Challenge 2003: Top Marketplace and Management Issues" (2003).

2. RHR International, "Filling the Executive Bench: How Companies Are Growing Future Leaders," White Paper (2005).

3. Corporate Leadership Council, *Building the High Performance Workforce: A Quantitative Analysis of the Effectiveness of Performance Management Strategies* (Washington D.C.: Corporate Executive Board, 2002).

4. Conference Board.

5. Accenture, *Accenture High Performance Workforce Study* (2004), p. 6.

6. Accenture, *Accenture High Performance Workforce Study* (2006), p. 21.

7. Corporate Leadership Council, *Hallmarks of Leadership Success: Strategies for Improving Leadership Quality and Executive Readiness* (Washington, D.C.: Corporate Executive Board, 2003), p. x.

8. P. Drucker, "Managing Oneself," *Harvard Business Review* (March-April 1999).

9. Personal conversation with Dean Walsh, Managing Director, Sullivan-Walsh Associates, Arlington Heights, Ill., July 31,2007.

10. P. Drucker, *The Effective Executive* (New York: HarperCollins, 2006).

11. Ibid, p. 18.

12. M. Buckingham and C. Coffman, *First, Break All the Rules* (New York: Simon & Schuster, 1999), p. 141.

13. Corporate Leadership Council, *Hallmarks of Leadership Success: Strategies for Improving Leadership Quality and Executive Readiness.* Washington D.C.: Corporate Executive Board (2003), p. 39b.

14. R. Gandossy and M. Effron, *Leading the Way: Three Truths from the Top Companies for Leaders* (Hoboken, N.J.: John Wiley & Sons, 2004).

15. M. Guthridge, A. Komm, and E. Lawson, "The People Problem in Talent Management," *McKinsey Quarterly*, Number 2 (2006).

16. Corporate Leadership Council, *High-Impact Succession Management: Accelerating Executive Development,* Chapter II (Washington, D.C.: Corporate Executive Board, 2003).

17. Corporate Leadership Council , *Hallmarks of Leadership Success* (2003).

18. Corporate Leadership Council, *High-Impact Succession Management,* pp. 45–49.

19. H. Handfield-Jones, "How Executives Grow," *McKinsey Quarterly,* Number 1 (2000).

20. M. McCall, *High Flyers* (Boston: Harvard Business School Press, 1998).

21. M. Goldsmith, "Foreword," in R. Gandossy and M. Effron, eds., *Leading the Way* (Hoboken, N.J.: John Wiley & Sons, 2004), p. ix.

*Chapter Six*

# Key Position Excellence

*"When people in key positions outperform their competitor peers, we win."*

B usiness success is largely a result of outperforming competitors in areas that are most important to customers and shareholders. The authors of the two most comprehensive studies of how companies create sustained competitive advantage agree: Great companies become great by relentlessly driving performance improvements in a few select areas. Jim Collins of *Good to Great* fame (the author of one of the comprehensive studies referred to earlier) writes: "Much of the answer to the question of 'good to great' lies in the discipline to do whatever it takes to become the best within carefully selected areas and then to seek continual improvements from there."[1]

William Joyce, Nitin Nohria, and Bruce Roberson—the authors of *What Really Works*, discussed in Chapter 4 (the other comprehensive study)—found the same relationship: "Winners recognized that there was no way they could be truly flawless, outperforming competitors on all operating parameters. Instead, they determined which processes were most important to meeting customers' expectations and focused their energies and resources on making these processes as efficient and productive as possible."[2]

The principal lesson from these important studies is that great companies identify the most critical levers for business success and build systems for continually improving performance on each lever. This is not new thinking. In the 1950s, when industrial companies drove global economic growth, W. Edwards Deming introduced an integrated, measured, and disciplined system for improving manufacturing performance. He stated: "A system is a network of components that work together to try to accomplish the aim of the system. A system must have an aim. Without an aim, there is no system. The aim of the system must be clear to everyone in the system."[3]

An automobile engine is a system. The generic aim of automobile engines is to propel a car and its contents as cost effectively as possible. To accomplish its aim, an engine needs a network of component parts that work together to move the automobile. This network of parts—the system—must be clear to all who work on the engine.

To Deming, the aim—also called "consistency of purpose"—was the foundational step. Only after this purpose was set could a system be designed to "improve, constantly and forever, the system of production." Deming's philosophy, now deeply ingrained in the world's manufacturing profession, is equally applicable for proactively building competitive advantage in people-intensive organizations. No different from improving manufacturing performance, a system for improving human capital performance begins with a constant purpose and a network of components (i.e., not a collection of programs) that improve, constantly and forever, the system of production.

The purpose of the New Human Capital Strategy is to systematically improve performance on a selected set of corporate core competencies. We have addressed executive team and leadership performance in the preceding chapters. This chapter discusses how to systematically improve the performance of employees who most heavily impact corporate core competency performance.

## Key Position Performance: The Current State

Over the past few decades, the field of training and development has experienced an explosion of new products, programs, and human learning technologies. Think of the money and time that your company spends on employee training. Does training in your organization improve performance? Do management development courses reliably improve management performance? Accenture's 2006 High Performance Workforce Study found that only 3 percent of CEOs and 4 percent of CFOs are very satisfied with their corporate learning function.[4] In fact, across all executives surveyed, only 10 percent indicated that they were very satisfied with training, down from 15 percent in 2004. The Accenture study concluded: "Training has not evolved to the point at which it is providing the kind of support necessary to build and sustain superior workforces that can help companies become high-performance businesses." The answer to the question "Does it work?" is "Not real well."

Hard data from the Corporate Leadership Council confirms these perceptions.[5] The CLC analyzed data from various training programs to isolate the factors that improved workforce productivity. The research showed that the following types of training improved performance by less than 1 percent:

- Customer service training
- Sales training
- Quality control training
- Diversity training
- Leadership training
- New employee orientation
- New product training
- Process management training
- Technical training

Maybe that is why CEOs and CFOs are so dissatisfied—they sense that training investments are not improving business performance. Why is it that as training technologies become ever more sophisticated, satisfaction with training continues to fall? Three reasons come to mind.

## Why Is There Dissatisfaction with Training?

**Reason #1: Performance Improvements Require a System.** As previously mentioned, human capital performance improvements are only possible by improving system performance; it is rarely possible to achieve meaningful performance improvements through programs. HR subprofessions have made tremendous technical improvements over the past decades: better assessment centers, training programs, and e-learning modules. However, these programs and tools are like nonintegrated parts of an engine—an engine that has never been fully designed. Program designers continue to focus on making their engine part the best it can possibly be rather than focusing on improving the performance of the system.

The industrial analog is the component manufacturer who says, "I'm accountable for values and crankshafts. Whether the pistons work is not my problem." It's no different with human capital. Think of the HR manager who says, "Sales manager tools and information? That's not HR's problem." The aim of customers and shareholders is more productive employees, but that is rarely the aim of the HR or training staff. Their aim is best-in-class parts.

Performance improvements require a clearly defined aim and a disciplined system for delivering that aim. Fragmented and nonsystematic approaches may be necessary, but they are not sufficient for producing results. We need to begin with a common aim. As Deming said: "A system must be managed. It will not manage itself. Left to themselves in the Western world, components become selfish, competitive, independent profit centers. The secret is cooperation between components toward the aim of the organization. We cannot afford the destructive effects of competition."[6]

**Reason #2: Training Is Focused on Internal Customers.** In most training organizations, success is defined by programs that meet the internal customers' requests rather than by results that are valued by external customers. Think of a physician who does precisely what the patient says, whether the patient is right or not. Or think of the auto mechanic whose customer says, "My car is underperforming. I want you to put these new pistons in." What is the responsibility of the auto mechanic? Is it to do what the customer asks, whether the customer is right or not, or is it to improve the performance of the car?

I recently spoke to the COO of an Asian telecom company. He said, "We are in the middle of a revenue shortfall that has become a crisis. If we cannot fix it immediately, there will be very serious consequences. We need great leadership to pull us through." The COO's aim was to dig the company out of its revenue shortfall. He directed his HR leader to begin leadership training in earnest. The COO wanted to get my thoughts on a university program the HR leader had identified. The HR leader was internally focused and program-based. He did precisely what his customer (the COO) asked. The HR leader's aim was to deliver a world-class leadership program.

I asked the COO why he believed leadership was the problem. He said that sales managers were not disciplined, "What do you mean by that?" I asked. He said that they were not using the company's new sales pipeline process to manage opportunities. When I asked why they were not using it, he said that he was not sure. We brainstormed for a few minutes to diagnose the real cause:

- Was the pipeline management process poorly designed?
- Did the sales managers know how to use it?
- Did the sales managers' managers insist on using it?
- Did the sales managers believe it would help them be more successful?
- Was the process well-integrated with other sales systems?

The answer to each question was, "We are not sure." We all agreed that the next step was to conduct a root cause analysis rather than to evaluate university-based training programs.

How likely was it that the business crisis would have been resolved through the university leadership development course? Whose fault would it have been when the business did not turn around? And what is the responsibility of an HR/training leader? Is it to do what the internal customer asks, or is it to improve the performance of the business?

As the 2006 Accenture study noted, "A surprisingly low percentage of companies are focusing their training efforts primarily on business-oriented goals." More often than not, annual training plans are bottoms-up–generated plans for delivering generic, externally sourced "best practice" programs. Success is measured by the size of the training catalogue, number of attendees, and internal customer satisfaction. If internal customers are happy, then external customers will be happy too, right? Maybe not.

Let's look at a typical corporate university. Many corporate universities operate as cost centers that charge tuition to attending students. Their aim is to fully recover the costs of their facility and faculty and keep the lights on for another year. Corporate universities, like any other business, achieve this by creatively driving demand. In other words, they give internal customers what they want. Corporate university administrators know that classes held at nice locations sell better. A class on stress management in Aspen, Colorado during ski season will likely be a big seller; however, the likelihood that students will attend all class days is low. Additionally, administrators also know that students tend to take courses in areas where they are most accomplished rather than in areas where they need to fill critical skill gaps. Whether or not these tactics increase shareholder or external customer satisfaction is interesting, but keeping the lights on is the university's aim. Is it any wonder that training is seen as misaligned with business goals?

**Reason #3: Few Companies Have Data to Measure and Manage System Performance.** It is not possible to build and manage a system for improving human capital until there is valid performance data at the individual or team level. Think about today's financial management systems. Most corporate finance professionals can isolate financial performance (e.g., revenue, cost) at very low levels. They know, for example, that although software sales accounts for 10 percent of sales volume, they deliver 60 percent of gross profits, and that Japan accounts for 50 percent of those profits. They also know that selling IT solutions to banks accounts for 70 percent of Japan's software profits. Thus, producing and selling better software products to Japanese banks is the most important thing to get right to achieve the profit plan. This kind of data-centric, top-down approach is commonplace in finance. This approach enables an organization to effectively isolate problems and identify its few critical leverage points. This is possible not only because finance is externally focused and results-based, but because it uses unambiguous measures of performance that it can track deep into the organization.

Now think about today's most commonly measured human capital metrics. Many are collected at levels too high to identify variability and associated causes. For example, pulse surveys are becoming more popular. These surveys measure employee satisfaction on an eight-week cycle by sampling 3 to 5 percent of employees. The benefit is that companies shorten the feedback cycle to eight weeks; the drawback is that it is impossible to diagnose problems with a 5 percent sample. A 5 percent sample renders managers with ten direct reports invisible. Even for managers with one hundred people in their organization, a sample size of three to five is often too few to learn anything about their organization. The result is that managers do not know if they are at fault for falling scores or what they can do to get better. Too often, there is no response.

In many cases, employee turnover is similarly collected at too high a level. Consider measuring and managing turnover at a bank. In a retail banking unit, 100 percent turnover may be at industry standards. In the investment banking unit, turnover in excess of 10 percent may be disruptive. What does it mean when average bank turnover moves from 30 percent to 35 percent in a twelve-month period? Nothing. In addition, an overall turnover statistic does not tell us whether high or low performers are leaving or whether people were involuntarily managed out or voluntarily resigned. "What" may be known at a high level, but "why" may not be known at all.

The most important data for building and running a system for improving human capital is valid performance data at the lowest possible level. For those in team-based positions, the lowest level might be at the team-level. For others, it might be at an individual level. Accessing this data should be easy, since every employee has a performance appraisal rating. Or is it easy? Do you believe that appraisal ratings in your company are valid measures of performance? Your employees don't. In fact, a Corporate Leadership Council study of 19,000 employees in thirty-four countries found: "In the average company in the survey, an overwhelming 88 percent of employees feel that most people in their organization do not receive the performance ratings they deserve."[7]

No matter of sophisticated statistical analyses can transform impure performance data into meaningful information—garbage in, garbage out. Simply stated, if performance measures are impure, it will be impossible to use the data to measure true year-over-year changes or to use the data to learn from experience to make better human capital decisions.

Improving performance for those in key positions not only requires valid performance data, but also an integrated performance improvement system and organizational capabilities to build and run the system. The following case study, from AT&T Global Services, provides a blueprint of what success might look like.

## Improving Performance of Those in Key Positions: A Case Study

In the late 1990s technology boom, AT&T Global Services, AT&T's business unit that sold to its largest corporate customers, realigned its sales force. Previously, sales representatives sold a broad array of AT&T voice and data products and services. However, as telecommunication technologies shifted from voice to data networking, AT&T customers began to complain that their internal IT staff members not only knew more than AT&T sales reps about new telecommunications technologies, but they also knew more than their AT&T sales reps about many of AT&T's new products and services. When questioned, Global Services sales reps agreed with its customers' assessment. In response, the Global Services executive team realigned its sales and marketing organizations into vertically integrated product/service lines—Data, Call Centers, Voice, Internet Protocol, etc. Sales reps went from selling all AT&T business products to selling just products within a single product/service line—Call Center Sales Specialists, Voice Sales Specialists, Internet Protocol Sales Specialists, etc.

To provide information and support for these new specialized roles, Pat Traynor, AT&T Global Services vice president of marketing, created Knowledge Communities for each product/service line. The purpose of each Knowledge Community was to deliver product/service line business plans by: (1) coordinating members and activities from the top of each value chain to the bottom (i.e., product development to sales), and (2) systematically improving human capital.

Each Knowledge Community was led by a Knowledge Community facilitator team of three to four full-time people. The Knowledge Community facilitator team reported hardline to Traynor but also worked closely with the AT&T Global Services head of HR and training (see Figure 6-1). Every product development, marketing, technical sales, and sales professional was aligned to a single Knowledge Community, but each still reported hardline to his/her assigned function. For example, Data Sales Specialists in Atlanta received all information, tools, and support to sell effectively from the Data Knowledge Community, but they formally reported to an Atlanta sales leader who conducted weekly sales pipeline reviews and was responsible for annual appraisals.

Knowledge Community facilitator teams operated in much the same way as the brand manager model mentioned in Chapter 5: They were the integrators who were accountable for sales performance to plan for a given product/service line. Facilitator team leaders had almost no formal authority, but they had substantial informal authority.

*Figure 6-1. The AT&T Global Services Knowledge Community structure.*

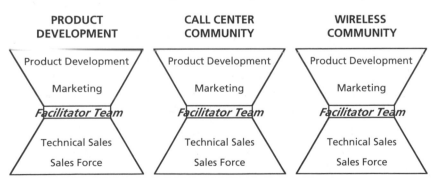

These brand manager–type teams were organized on the following principles:

- *Line-Owned.* Knowledge Community facilitation was not an HR role although HR programs were important. Neither was it a marketing communications role although moving information up and down the value chain (i.e., from product development to sales) was a critical task. The community facilitation role was owned by functions directly accountable for financial results.

- *Results-Based Focus.* The purpose of the Knowledge Community facilitation team was to improve business performance for its assigned community by ensuring that community members outperformed those in competitor organizations. A precondition for performance excellence is superior talent and skills, but that alone cannot create competitive advantage. Outperforming peers at competitor organizations not only requires capable people but capable people with the right motivation, information, tools, manager, etc. Knowledge Community performance was assessed by a lagging indicator—industry-best performance. Industry-best people was a necessary, but not sufficient, condition.

- *Community Coordinator.* Before the Knowledge Communities were set up, not only were HR programs uncoordinated, but so too were programs between and within product development, marketing, communications, and IT. No function had taken a leadership role for designing a blueprint of success (i.e., what the house looks like when it's done) or for building a system for getting there. Consequently, each department was, with the best of intentions, producing programs and tools that seemed important for business success. The Knowledge Community facilitator team's brand management role filled this leadership gap. The facilitator team was accountable for: (1) designing a blueprint for success, (2) building a top-down, integrated system for delivering that blueprint, and (3) "constantly and forever" improving the performance of that system.

The facilitator team mandate was to deliver long-term profitable revenue growth by ensuring that Global Services sales reps outperformed competitor reps. This became each community's lagging indicator and was measured at a sales rep level using existing market research survey that asked customers to compare the quality of Global Services reps with those of other telecom providers. This customer rating was attached to the performance records of each national account manager and to the performance record of each account team member.

The system for growing community capabilities and performance was similar across Knowledge Communities. For each community, the system for achieving the lagging indicator of better-than-competitor performance required excellence in five system components (see Figure 6-2,) These five components were chosen as most important for ensuring that Global Services reps outperform competitor reps. If any one was subpar, there would be little chance of success. However, if performance on each was strong, AT&T would have a competitive advantage.

The first component was to build a subsystem that finds, selects, and maintains top talent. Success required hiring and keeping the industry's best and making sure that there were enough people to fill the open seats. *Metrics: Percent staffed, average time from hire to quota, percent at quota, turnover of those at quota, etc.*

The second component was to create best-in-industry skills. Skills are different from talent. Being a talented 6'10" athlete is great, but you

*Figure 6-2. The AT&T Global Services Knowledge Community system components.*

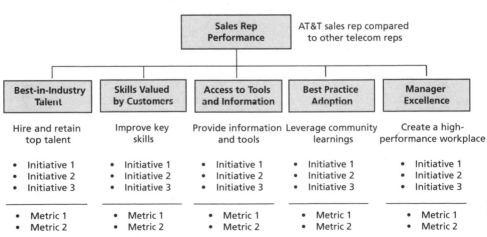

need to know how to dribble and shoot a basketball to be a successful player. So it is with sales reps. AT&T not only needed industry-best talent but it needed to ensure that the talent had industry-best technical knowledge and sales skills. Knowledge Community facilitator teams identified the most important skills and results for individual revenue growth and partnered with the training organization to create prescriptive learning plans around those results. All other training programs were eliminated. Notice that this is a top-down, results-based approach to employee development. *Metrics: Year-over-year improvements in sales skills, year-over-year improvements in technical test scores.*

The third component was to ensure that all community members had access to tools and information. Having highly talented people with good technical skills was great, but customers would not be impressed if these people did not have access to product or process information and did not know of the company's offerings. A customer question of "Do you think Cisco's new router will work with our current system?" could not be answered with, "I don't know. Does Cisco have a new router?" Real-time access to information was critical.

Each Knowledge Community facilitator team created a website that held virtually all information and tools needed to sell its products and solutions. Had HR run the communities, it is unlikely that this would have been chosen as a critical success factor; tools and information are outside HR's traditional scope of activities. Yet sales rep performance requires both tools and information; performance requires a fully integrated system.

Mass e-mails from corporate employees to "the field" were stopped and replaced by a messaging system that filtered and edited communications and placed them on the Knowledge Community website. After years of following a routine of doing business through e-mails, many reps insisted they would not use the website. How did the Knowledge Community facilitator team handle the delicate issue of change management? They stopped all e-mail information exchanges from headquarters to the field. When resisters became sufficiently hungry for information, they came to the website. *Metrics: Number of unique users per week to Knowledge Community websites, number of hits per day, activity surveys of time spent looking for information, etc.*

The fourth component was best practice adoption. Best practice sharing is an activity; adoption is a result. This is different from importing best practice programs from other companies. High levels of performance variance between employees indicates that there are people who use current processes to deliver excellent performance. Rather than importing a new system from another company, facilitator teams searched for and adopted methods that worked well in the current system. *Metrics: Financial impact of adopted practices by Knowledge Community, etc.*

Finally, the fifth component was manager excellence. Nothing works without great managers. *Metrics: Sales Manager key result changes, manager effectiveness surveys.*

## Key Position Excellence: The Roadmap

AT&T Global Services Knowledge Communities provides a blueprint of a system—a picture of what success looks like—for improving performance of those in key positions. The roadmap presented in Figure 6-3 is a more tactical methodology for getting from here to there.

*Figure 6-3. The Human Capital Management model.*

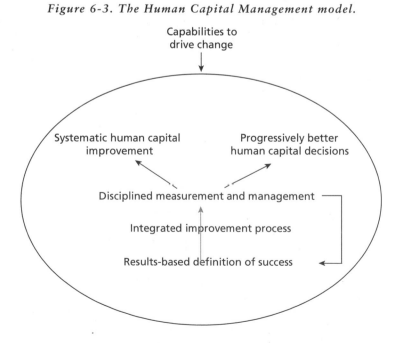

This roadmap follows the four steps of the Human Capital Management model.

## Building Capabilities to Drive Change

Today's silo-based organizations are not aligned for system performance improvements. Someone has to own and manage the system. At AT&T Global Services, the Knowledge Community facilitator team became the system leader. At consumer product companies, that role goes to brand managers. Don't begin the performance improvement journey until the organizational capabilities and accountabilities are in place to drive system performance improvements over time.

## Results-Based Definition of Success

As previously mentioned, study after study has identified the most important variable for improving employee performance as employees' understanding of what is expected of them. Make the goal crystal clear to all and align the organization to that goal, and performance will reliably improve. However, in many cases, that "clear understanding of what is expected"—the end-state measure—is not entirely clear.

Choosing lagging indicators for each key position is the first step. For professions like sales, choosing a lagging indicator (e.g., percent quota) is relatively easy. For others, like animators, it is far more difficult. Yet for each key position, a clearly defined and measured lagging indicator is (or indicators are) the critical first step. Let's take animators. Maybe the indicator is character cuteness as measured by focus groups or by a panel of internal colleagues. Any performance result can be measured. Here is an approach for creating a results-based definition of success for those in key roles.

**Step 1: Define Performance Outcomes.** Performance outcomes, or lagging indicators, begin with the business strategy or annual plan and cascade down. For each key position, the question is: "What is the most important thing for those in this key position to deliver, and what is the most objective way to measure that?" Remember that performance levels of those in key positions need not be world-class; they only need to exceed the performance of those in similar positions in competitor organizations. In the 1980s, MCI's strategy was to beat AT&T

in the courts through deregulation. At that time, MCI's attorneys occupied a key position. MCI's lawyers did not need to be better than their peers at Standard Oil. They needed only to be better than AT&T's lawyers.

**Step 2: Identify Key Results That Must Be Delivered to Achieve Performance Outcomes.** More often than not, managers of those in key positions have unarticulated thoughts about the most important things to do to achieve the performance outcome, but they have not created or documented these thoughts into a clear set of activities and results. A plan is not a plan until it is written. A few years ago, I had a discussion with John, a high-level partner at a private equity firm. I met with John in the biggest executive suite I had ever seen—a three-story-high office atop a high-rise office building in downtown Tokyo. John was frustrated with managers in a large Japanese financial institution that his company had recently acquired. He said, "The problem is that these employees refuse to accept the new way." I said, "John, in thirty seconds or less, what is the new way?" He went silent, then smiled coyly and said, "You're right. If I can't explain it, they can't accept it." John and his team had not defined the key results for those in key positions—the results most important for achieving the performance outcomes. Until he did, there would be a continual push-pull between managers and employees as each worked off a different assumption set.

**An Effective Results-Based Definition of Success: A Case Study.** The Chief Sales Officer of a U.S. telecom company had been preaching for years that sales reps must shift from selling single products to selling bundled solutions. Sales leaders gave many speeches, changed compensation plans, and required sales reps to attend solution selling courses. However, neither the number of bundled products sold nor the customer perception that the company sold useful solutions had changed. All members of the sales function knew *who* they needed to be, but not *what* they needed to do to get there. Eventually, the company decided to change its approach to a results-based sales model that defined five key results required to be a successful solution seller—what reps must do to sell solutions. That model is presented in Table 6-1.

Table 6-1. National account manager key results.

| Key Results | Level 1 Results | Level 2 Results | Level 3 Results |
|---|---|---|---|
| 1. Earn client's respect as a business partner | • Is a trusted partner to the telecom manager, and meets periodically with the CIO.<br>• NAM has positioned some of our senior team members with client executives.<br>• We are typically asked to propose on, and are given a fair chance to win. | • Is established as a trusted contributor to client's top executives (CIO and higher) and to client's functional and business unit leaders.<br>• Has effectively positioned GSM, SCVP, RVP, and ACE officer throughout the account.<br>• If everything is equal, client chooses us. | • NAM is established as a trusted adviser to the client's team of top executives.<br>• NAM has effectively positioned GSM, SCVP, RVP, and ACE officer in the account.<br>• If everything is close, client chooses us. |
| 2. Conduct account planning and forecasting | • Business plan expectations are shared with and accepted by customer and virtual team members. Examples:<br>1. NAM uses plan as a day-to-day working document<br>2. Virtual team members prioritize their work according to the plan | • Business plan expectations are shared with and accepted by customer and virtual team members, and at least one client business plan is used as a best practice example for other NAMs. | • NAM is sought by others to make improvements in the client business management/forecasting process. |
| 3. Sell state-of-the-art applications that solve client needs | • Continued revenue growth.<br>• Efficient use of our selling resources. Examples:<br>1. Brings in appropriate resources at the appropriate time.<br>2. Does not hoard internal resources.<br>3. Plans effectively.<br>• Sells applications that solve client needs. | • Continued revenue growth overall and in emerging technologies at expected level.<br>• NAM achieves excellent morale on virtual teams and high levels of productivity.<br>• Client executives recognize that NAM has helped improve the client's business results (e.g., increased speed or reduced cost in a core process). | • Continued and revenue growth substantially above expected level and in emerging technologies.<br>• Turnkey solutions for customers that draw upon a wide range of external suppliers.<br>• NAM has helped shape client's business strategy in a meaningful way. |
| 4. Manage day-to-day client activities in a proactive and professional manner | • As a result of regular shared expectations meetings and stewardship reviews, telecom staff understands our deliverables to date and short-term plans.<br>• Customer holds clear and reasonable expectations of team (e.g., accepts our intervals). | • As a result of regular shared expectations meetings and stewardship reviews with CIO, customer understands our results to date and short-term plans.<br>• Efficiently uses our service and support resources.<br>• Customer satisfaction score on responsiveness measures of at least 70 in two consecutive quarters. | • As a result of regular shared expectations meetings and stewardship reviews with CEO/COO, customer understands the results we delivered to date and short-term plans.<br>• Customer satisfaction score on responsiveness above 80 for two consecutive quarters.<br>• Frequently used as a role model in managing day-to-day activities efficiently and effectively from GS, Customer Care, and client perspectives. |
| 5. Serve as an effective team member within the sales center | • Regularly adopts best practices shared by others.<br>• Stays current on information shared through the sales center through collaboration with other NAMs. | • NAM's best practices are replicated quickly in the sales center, region, etc.<br>• Helps achieve shorter learning curve for new NAMs by using knowledge/skills to assist other NAMs. Peers seek NAM out for collaboration. | • NAM's best practices are replicated quickly throughout the company.<br>• Is viewed by peers and clients as a vertical market networking expert. Develops innovative approaches, products, and services. |

The activities listed in the "Key Results" column were considered the five most important things to get right for reps to sell solutions and achieve personal revenue targets. This set of key results formed the foundation for a systematic, disciplined, and measured approach to year-over-year performance improvements in the sales rep position. The benefits of this approach were:

- *A Clear Set of Expectations.* Clear expectations are the most important variable for performance improvement. This became the performance contract between the manager and employee.

- *The Manager and the Employee on the Same Side.* The manager was not forced to play judge or rank employees against one another. He/she had the same goal as the reps: move everyone from Level 1 to Level 3.

- *Sales Rep Perception of a Fair Assessment.* The rep either met with the telecom manager or he/she did not. There were far fewer hard feelings from those who received poor ratings.

- *Year-Over-Year Performance Improvements That Are Known and Managed at the Individual Level.* Organizational leaders finally knew whether their rep performance was improving year-over-year and why.

- *Ability to Learn from Experience.* Not only were year-over-year changes known, but by capturing data at an individual level, human capital decisions were analyzed and improved by using past experience. For example, by correlating performance data for each key result with selection test data, the company was able to learn which selection tools were the best predictor of selling excellence.

## Comprehensive and Integrated Development

Think of development not as training but as a system that produces consistent improvements in the performance outcome of incumbents in a key position. The system designer has a brand manager–type role as described earlier in this chapter. Once the brand manager strikes an agreement with stakeholders on performance outcomes and key result measures, he/she needs to craft a focused, prescriptive development plan for driving improvements on each key result. Development plan design may include the following steps:

- Assess current performance at the individual/team level.
- Identify performance gaps and root causes.
- Create plans to close gaps.
- Measure changes and redefine approach.

**Step 1: Assess Current Performance at the Individual/Team Level.** Let's stay with the sales rep example. In many U.S. companies, the national account manager (NAM) is the lead sales rep for a large account. (NAMs may manage people, but often they do not.) A common performance outcome for a NAM is "percent quota attainment." Performance on this lagging measure is easily assessed by current financial systems. Many sales managers attempt to grow sales by managing quota attainment—by pushing harder. A more effective method is to measure and monitor lagging indicators and manage leading indicators—key results.

Performance on key result metrics may be more difficult to collect as this data may reside in various corporate databases such as customer satisfaction databases, HR information warehouses, and financial systems. The first task is to determine baseline performance for each NAM on performance outcomes and key results.

**Step 2: Identify Performance Gaps and Root Causes.** Next, look at performance variance across NAMs. If performance outcome averages are below competitors (e.g., revenue per rep) and performance variance is low (i.e., reps all sell roughly the same amount), the problem is likely to be with the business process or the job design. If the variance is wide, the problem is more likely to be a capability one.

Deming taught that performance variability in areas most critical to business success poses a significant threat to long-term business performance; the greater the variability in performance outcomes, the

*Figure 6-4. Identifying performance variability.*

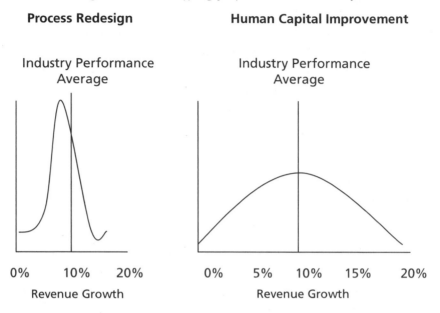

higher the operating costs. Look at Figure 6-4. Let's say these charts represent NAM performance on the performance outcome revenue growth. The *y*-axis represents the number of NAMs with that revenue growth score. The *x*-axis represents different levels of revenue growth.

The left-hand graph in Figure 6-4 indicates that performance variability between reps is narrow. Almost all reps have year-over-year revenue growth of between 2 percent and 15 percent, and the average performance level of 8 percent growth is below the industry average growth of 10 percent. Low performance variability means that performance is roughly similar across reps: They likely understand and follow the process in similar ways. If most employees follow the process in the same way, but the average output of the process is below industry averages, the sales process or product may be at fault.

The right-hand graph in Figure 6-4 depicts wide performance variability. Applying the same process/tools, some NAMs can sell well above industry norms while others cannot. This performance variability may be caused by manager support, tenure in position, talent to do the job, skill training, unequal access to information, etc. Bottom line: When you see high-performance variability, think human capital opportunity.

The next analysis helps determine whether the key results you selected really are predictive of your performance outcome—in this case, revenue growth. Look at Figure 6-5. The data suggests that four of the five key results are good predictors—four are big numbers; one is small (i.e., 12). Except for sales center leadership, we chose good leading indicators. There is no reason to create developmental opportunities for sales center leadership as that is not predictive of the quota attainment. Eliminate that key result and replace it with another. For the four key results that are good predictors, identify where there are gaps and why. Starting with nine key results and ending with a list of five of the most powerful predictors of sales growth is better than beginning with five and ending with two.

Notice that the global sales model in the figure uncovered four key results at the global level, but when the data was cut by country, a different sales model emerged. The data suggests that in Japan, sales center leadership is very important, but executive selling is not at all related to quota attainment. It appears that successful selling in Japan happens at a lower organizational level than in other countries. Creating a globally consistent sales model that requires NAM excellence in executive positioning will confuse Japanese NAMs and frustrate Japanese customers. Customers and managers should expect relationship excellence in lower-level relationships. But global corporate edicts on the importance of executive positioning, sales assessments, and training force accountability for higher-level relationships will

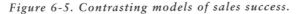

*Figure 6-5. Contrasting models of sales success.*

push NAMs in the wrong direction. This situation is very common in global companies today. Conceptually, the one-size-fits-all model sounds great, but it may not always be what customers need.

**Step 3: Create Plans to Close Gaps.** All training and development opportunities, business reviews, and sales tools should be explicitly designed to close key result performance gaps. Certainly, some sales reps may need special development to overcome specific weaknesses—for example, time management or sensitivity training. These should be viewed as exceptions and sent to coaches or courses outside the traditional training system. The core development engine must focus on improving performance on one or more key results for each key position.

The objective of a results-based development plan is to strengthen performance on key results. The brand manager must build an integrated system that reliably delivers year-over-year performance improvements on each key result. Consider the system components used in the Knowledge Community example presented earlier:

- Hire and keep best-in-industry talent.
- Ensure best-in-industry knowledge and skills.
- Provide access to tools and information.
- Adopt best practices.
- Ensure that managers focus and motivate employees.

Consider crafting one to three performance measures for each component. Then, define the programs, activities, and deliverables in support of each component quarter-by-quarter. The first week of the new quarter may be a good time for an accountability review on programs and deliverables, a check of key performance metrics if available, and commitments for next-quarter deliverables.

**Step 4: Measure Changes and Redefine Approach.** How can you know if your development approach is adding real value to customers and shareholders? In other words, does it work? Just look at year-over-year changes to the key results, position by position. For example:

- Did NAMs grow revenue faster this year than last year?
- How did the average person score on each of the five key results?
- Which results showed strong improvement? How did variance by result change?
- Which sales managers grew NAM key results fastest? What did they do?

In addition to knowing that performance improved, understanding why it improved is also important. Correlating performance changes between each key result and each development activity provides insight into how influential each activity was to each key result. It answers the question, "Did it work?" Figure 6-6 shows how this is done. The key result examined here is planning and forecasting. Developmental activities that were related to improved account planning and forecasting appear to be business reviews, peer mentoring, and coaching. Neither workshop appears to be related to planning and forecasting improvements.

As a behavioral scientist, I feel obligated to point out that these are correlations and do not imply causality: However, in many cases causality may exist.

## Measure and Manage

Several years ago, I was playing golf with two friends, both physicians. One said to the other, "I have to buckle down and study for my licensing exam. I was supposed to take it six months ago, but I got a deferment, and I just took a second deferment, but that's my last one.

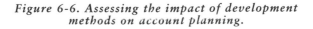

*Figure 6-6. Assessing the impact of development methods on account planning.*

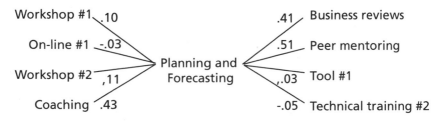

Workshop #1 .10       .41 Business reviews

On-line #1 -.03       .51 Peer mentoring

Planning and Forecasting

Workshop #2 .11       .03 Tool #1

Coaching .43       -.05 Technical training #2

If I don't recertify next month, I can't practice medicine anymore."
"What a difference in perspective between physicians and corporate
workers when it comes to learning," I thought. The learning paradigm
in medicine is results-based: You are accountable for passing recertifi-
cation tests or you stop practicing. The model we use in business is different: Think of high-potential development programs where course
attendance is tracked, but leadership performance changes are not.

As a leader of the training organization at AT&T Global Services,
I wondered what the medical paradigm would look like in a corporate
setting. What if we said, "I don't care if you come to training, and if
you do, I don't care if you like it. All I care about is that your technical
capabilities exceed a defined threshold and improve every year." This is
somewhat exaggerated to make a point. We do want people to feel their
time in training was well spent, but should we really care if they come
to training?

Our training team at AT&T flipped the paradigm from program-
based to results-based through annual technical tests. As you will recall from the start of this chapter, AT&T customers were frustrated
with the technical skills offered by their sales representatives. There
was little chance of AT&T reps becoming business advisers when their
clients knew more about technologies and products than they did. To
solve this business problem, we decided to run mandatory technical
tests each October. Each Knowledge Community facilitator team created a test for its community members—a Call Center test for Call
Center Knowledge Community members, etc. We decided to carry
over 20 percent of the questions from the previous year's test to the
new test in order to answer the question "Are our Call Center members more technically capable this year than last year?"

In the fall of the first year, all 4,500 AT&T Global Services sales representatives took a technical test for their assigned Knowledge Community. We totaled all of the scores by sales center. We then ranked every
sales center by score and sent the results out to everyone. VPs with high
rankings were very proud of their results and wanted to make sure their
technical skills would stay at the top in the following year.

Sales center vice presidents with low scores called in a panic, asking
for help. Few were surprised that their sales reps scored poorly; they had

been on joint sales calls with them and had also heard complaints from customers. But this was different. Their sales professionals were terribly upset. They had been telling their VPs for some time that they needed training, but seeing real results on paper cut them to the core. No one wants to believe that he is less than expert on his job. The day the scores were released, AT&T Global Services became a learning organization—an organization obsessed with development.

Within one week, all training classes sold out for the next six months—an important leading indicator of technical score improvements. The aim was now clear and focused and a system was in place to deliver results to that aim. When energy is infused into the system, results are inevitable. It took only a few months for customers to begin to notice the change. Customer satisfaction scores began to creep upward after years of decline and during a sustained decline of customer satisfaction with the industry.

Equally important was employee energy created by the new system. Among Global Services sales reps, satisfaction with training, as measured by the popular Mayflower survey, grew from 35 percent satisfied to 76 percent satisfied. The Mayflower Group is a consortium of companies that runs a job satisfaction survey (Mayflowergroup.org). That was a 41-point year-over-year improvement. Given that a 2-point improvement was statistically significant, this was a big result. Many shudder to think that HR/training would rank sales centers from smartest to dumbest and send it out for all to see; it seems cruel. But who is more cruel—the permissive parent who worries about meeting the child's current desires, or the parent who sets high standards and expects hard work and delayed gratification? A 41-point increase in training satisfaction and a 19-point increase with overall employment satisfaction (over twelve months) indicated that at AT&T, it was the latter.

**Measuring for Performance Improvements.** After you read this chapter, it should be clear what methods you can use for acquiring performance data for individuals in key positions. An effective tool for capturing and analyzing this data is a human capital database sorted by key position. Ideally, this would be done within the current HRIS

Table 6-2. Key position database using the
example of a national account manager.

Every sales manager's data
is input into the database

| ID | Mgr | Loc | HiPo | Tim pos | Key Results | | | Customer Satisfaction | | | Financial Results | | | Competencies | | | Training Workshop | | |
|---|---|---|---|---|---|---|---|---|---|---|---|---|---|---|---|---|---|---|---|
| | | | | | 1 | 2 | 3 | 1 | 2 | 3 | Qta | Rev | Expn | 1 | 2 | 3 | 1 | 2 | 3 |
| | | | | | | | | | | | | | | | | | | | |
| | | | | | | | | | | | | | | | | | | | |
| | | | | | | | | | | | | | | | | | | | |
| | | | | | | | | | | | | | | | | | | | |
| | | | | | | | | | | | | | | | | | | | |

database. This method is similar to the one introduced in Chapter 5 to measure and manage leadership performance. See Table 6-2.

Being able to sort the data can tell us key result changes by:

- *Manager.* Which manager is growing his/her people the fastest?

- *Region, Country, City.* Where are internal best practices?

- *High Potential.* Are high potentials growing faster than the norm?

- *Time in Key Position.* What is the relationship between time in position and performance?

Additional variables will help improve decision making. For example, adding sale rep scores from a selection tool administered before beginning the role will identify which assessment exercises are predictive of sales performance. Adding competency assessment scores helps us know whether competencies are more or less predictive of sales results than key results. Assessing competencies over time tells us which competencies change over time and which do not. Adding key developmental experiences tells us if high potentials are being stretched into new and different assignments or if they have been in only a few roles in their career. Bringing this type of data to the table enables HR and line managers to learn from experience to make progressively better human capital decisions.

Contrast this approach with the 2006 update to USC's Center for Effective Organizations study on HR. The authors note that "Rarely is HR measurement specifically directed to vital talent 'segments,'" and that "No measurement elements are used by more than 50 percent of responding organizations." Of organizations that did report using measures, those used most measure the efficiency of HR processes. The authors wrote: "Cost-benefit analysis has often been referred to as the 'Holy Grail' of HR measurement . . . . Understanding the ROI of HR programs is useful, but in doing so may tell little about the synergies among HR programs and the overall value of measures in enhancing decisions about human capital."[8]

The human capital measurement system is about measuring results across vital talent segments and using the data to make better human capital decisions. Capturing and analyzing the data is critically important. Now let's look at a few ways to use the data to infuse energy and accountability into the system.

**Managing for Performance Improvements.** The aim is now clear: We have defined end-state measures and key results by position. We know the performance gaps by key result. A system is now in place to drive performance improvements and close gaps on each key result. And a measurement system is collecting data to determine progress on those results over time. The last step for improving performance of those in key positions is to create an ongoing management system that infuses the system with energy. Creating this energy requires joint ownership and accountability by line managers and HR leaders through a jointly owned scorecard and regularly scheduled reviews.

Human capital scorecards have three levels: (1) end-state measure, (2) key results, and (3) projects and deliverables. Table 6-3 shows an example of the last two levels.

Using the NAM example, data for the scorecard might be generated by the person accountable for year-over-year NAM performance improvements. Quarterly reviews might be held with the

*Table 6-3. Sample human capital scorecard.*

| KEY RESULT | SCORE | | | PROJECTS | | |
|---|---|---|---|---|---|---|
| | CURRENT | GAP | DESIRED | PROJECT NAME | DELIVERABLE | DATE |
| 1. Executive Positioning | | | | | | |
| 2. Account Plan | | | | | | |
| 3. Sell Solutions | | | | | | |
| 4. Day-to-day actives | | | | | | |
| 5. Effective sales center member | | | | | | |

CEO/BU head/sales executive beginning with a summary of last quarter's results versus commitments set at the beginning of the quarter. The review ends with a new set of commitments for the upcoming quarter.

Annual reviews might be designed to present year-over-year changes on end-state measures and key results. Figure 6-7 shows how this might look. The next nine slides would show progress on each point.

*Figure 6-7. Sample format for a key position review.*

**Key Position Review:  National Account Manager**

1. Here is the performance of our NAMs versus performance of competitors for the last three years.
2. Here is what a 1 percent performance improvement is worth to revenue and profit for each NAM.
3. Here are the twelve-month performance changes for each of the five NAM key results.
4. Here is the customer and financial impact of those changes.
5. This is why average NAM performance changed.
6. Here are last year's investments for NAM key results.
7. Here is the impact of each program on key result performance.
8. Here is what we have learned from our experience so far and several changes we will make in the coming year.
9. Here are next year's performance improvement goals, planned investments, and expected ROI.

# Conclusion

Edwards Deming's paradigm shift in manufacturing performance was right. Aim, build a system to accomplish that aim, and then continually improve the system. Growing those in key positions is the same. By running annual assessments for multiple years and adding data to a human capital database, what can we know?

- The sales managers whose teams consistently deliver financial results
- The key results that are most predictive of financial results
- Sales manager performance on each key result
- Which sales executives have the most successful sales managers
- The impact of training workshops on key results
- The impact of time in position on key results
- The correlation of performance appraisal to key results
- The growth of high performers

When the COO talks to a regional sales executive, he/she will know how the sales managers in that executive's region are performing on each key result and how that compares with other regions.

Customer and financial results in companies with large numbers of people are largely a function of reducing performance variability of individuals or teams that occupy key positions. This requires a fine-tuned people management system that tracks objective measures of performance and, over time, uncovers the productivity drivers with the greatest impact:

- All development must be aligned to one or more key results.
- Performance improvement requires more than traditional training.
- The most important variable is clarity of expectations. The second is feedback and accountability for employees and their managers.

- One of the quickest ways to improve the average performance level and reduce variance is to move chronically low performers.

This system answers several important questions:

- How is success defined and measured for the target position?
- What are the three to five key results that have the greatest impact on that success?
- What is the economic value to performance improvements by those in a given key position?
- How is the performance of those in key positions changing year-over-year?

# Notes

1. J. Collins, *Good to Great: Why Some Companies Make the Leap . . . and Others Don't* (New York: HarperCollins, 2001), p. 128.

2. W. F. Joyce, N. Nohria, and B. Roberson, *What Really Works: The 4+2 Formula for Sustained Business Success* (New York: HarperCollins, 2003), pp. 122–123.

3. W. E. Deming, *The New Economics of Industry, Government, Education* (Cambridge, Mass.: MIT Press, 1993), p. 51.

4. Accenture, *Accenture High Performance Workforce Study* (2006), p. 71.

5. Corporate Leadership Council, *Building the High-Performance Workforce: A Quantitative Analysis of the Effectiveness of Performance Management Strategies* (Washington, D.C.: Corporate Executive Board, 2002), p. 43b.

6. W. E. Deming, *The New Economics of Industry, Government, Education* (Cambridge, Mass.: MIT Press, 1993), p. 51.

7. Corporate Leadership Council, "Performance Management System," in *Benchmarking the High-Performance Organization* (Washington D.C.: Corporate Executive Board, 2003), p. 20.

8. E. Lawler, J. Boudreau, and S. Mohrman, *Achieving Strategic Excellence: An Assessment of Human Resource Organizations* (Stanford, Calif.: Stanford University Press, 2006), p. 72.

*Chapter Seven*

# Improving Workforce Performance

*"What exactly is a high-performance organization
and how do you measure and manage it?"*

Jon and Karen Taylor are the parents of four children ranging from age 5 to 15. The Taylors take their parental duties seriously and strive to do their best to ensure that their children succeed in life.

It's December 30 and time for the children's annual performance appraisals. Sara, age 15, is the oldest and, as usual, the first to go.

JON: Sara, I know that you are anxious to know your annual rating, so let's get right to it. We ranked you third among your siblings and gave you a 2 on our family's 5-point scale.

SARA: But I thought you were proud of me.

JON: Sara, as you know, we have high standards in this house. A 2 is not so bad. If you work hard next year, you certainly might improve your score and rank.

SARA:    But what did I do wrong?

KAREN:   Well, for one thing, you neglected your chores at least five times this year. Just a minute, I have them documented right here. . . .

Sara:    But that was last February. I haven't missed my chores even once since then. I thought you forgave me for that.

Karen:   That may be true, but remember that this is an annual appraisal; February problems count.

How might this appraisal affect Sara? Will it accelerate her growth, performance, and confidence? Will it help her be a better big sister to her siblings? Will it strengthen the bond of trust and the free flow of information with her parents?

This example may seem absurd for a parent/child interaction. Why, then, are forced rankings, tough conversations, and the like considered necessary for building a high-performance workforce? At what point in the human life cycle do the scientific principles of human behavior do an about-face? The answer is: They don't.

In 2003, the Corporate Leadership Council conducted a study we have cited previously in this book. The study involved 19,000 employees in thirty-four organizations from seven industries and twenty-nine countries to find out which performance improvement activities and programs actually delivered performance improvements. The study began with 106 performance drivers and ranked each on its impact on performance. Table 7-1 summarizes the results. The first column presents the practices that have the biggest impact on performance. The second column is the percentage improvement in performance expected if you use that practice. The third column presents the drivers that are least important to driving performance, and the fourth column is the percentage performance change expected if you use that driver.

Look at the "Bottom Drivers" in the third column. Except for the last driver, they look suspiciously like "best practice performance management," don't they?

Think about these results as best and worst practices for raising children:

*Table 7-1. Best and worst performance drivers.*

| TOP DRIVERS | PERCENT IMPROVEMENT | BOTTOM DRIVERS | PERCENT IMPROVEMENT |
|---|---|---|---|
| Fairness and accuracy of feedback | +39.1 | Forced ranking | -.1 |
| Risk-taking culture | +38.9 | Increasing the number of formal reviews | -1.0 |
| Emphasis on strengths in appraisal | +36.4 | Emphasis in informal feedback on personality weaknesses | -3.2 |
| Understanding performance standards | +36.1 | Emphasis in appraisals on personality weaknesses | -5.5 |
| Internal communication | +34.4 | Emphasis in informal feedback on performance weaknesses | -10.9 |
| Manager knowledgeable about performance | +30.3 | Emphasis in appraisals on performance weaknesses | -26.8 |
| Opportunity to work on things you do best | +28.8 | Manager makes frequent changes | -27.8 |

- Do good parents encourage children to stretch and take risks?
- Do they emphasize strengths when giving feedback?
- Do children benefit from clear standards?
- Is communication important to helping them develop?
- Are good parents knowledgeable about their children's performance in sports, class, clubs, etc.?

It reads like good parenting in the first column ("Top Drivers") and child abuse in the third column ("Bottom Drivers"), doesn't it? Perhaps this is why managers are often resistant to do annual appraisals and why performance appraisals do not seem to improve motivation and confidence or strengthen the manager-employee relationship. If performance appraisals don't improve performance, why do we do them?

As you have read, the purpose of the Human Capital Strategy is to improve performance of corporate core competencies by creating and managing a system for improving performance of those in critical roles. So far, we have discussed how to improve performance in three critical roles: executive teams, leaders, and key positions. Think of these critical roles as good seeds. Good seeds need good soil—the larger organizational context within which these critical roles reside. This soil is often called the "high-performance organization." The purpose of this chapter is to create a blueprint for a high-performance organization and a roadmap to get there. This chapter is about good soil.

## Performance Improvement: The Current State

The important question to ask here is: *Does your company have a disciplined approach for improving workforce performance?* Remember in Chapter 3 when we discussed Accenture's 2004 High Performance Workforce Study? It found that improving worker productivity was the most important of thirteen identified HR issues, yet nineteen of twenty CEOs were less than very satisfied with their company's current performance.[1] Maybe corporate leaders are pushing the wrong levers. Which levers does your organization use? Does your organization have a workforce improvement plan that is measured and managed with discipline? Or does it rely on training and appraisals to improve performance?

Experienced consultants know that most client calls about performance concerns are founded on one or more of the following assumptions:

- Our people are unskilled. We need training.

- We continue to tolerate low performance. We need tougher appraisals.

A high-performance organization cannot be created by training and performance management alone. Each is a legitimate stand-alone part, but performance improvements require a system. Let's take a look at the current state of performance management systems.

The purist definition of performance management is a cycle that begins with goal setting and ends with compensation (see Figure 7-1.)

Nice theory, but for most people, performance management means performance appraisal. Appraisal systems are designed to increase productivity by pushing harder. They are based on the assumption that employees will work harder if they know there are consequences at year-end. As you will read in this chapter, research

*Figure 7-1. The performance management cycle.*

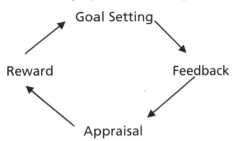

suggests that appraisals do not appear to have a significant positive impact on performance—no surprise since stand-alone parts cannot deliver performance improvements. Perhaps this is why they are redesigned so frequently: We assume that they are a valid tool for improving performance, yet we realize that they do not work.

## "Putting Teeth" in Performance Management

Several years ago, a Southeast Asian bank decided it wanted to create a "high-performance culture." At that time, the company's score on a popular employee survey question "People are rewarded according to their job performance" was five points above the cross-industry average (a one-point difference is statistically significant). However, the company decided to be proactive and push for even higher performance by "putting teeth" into the performance management process. The assumption was that high performance required a tough appraisal process that pushed employees harder, rewarded the winners, and punished the losers.

In the first year, the CHRO announced that the performance appraisal system would be "strengthened" through mandated rating distributions (i.e., 10 percent can get a 5 rating, 20 percent a 4, etc.). After years of stable ratings on the employee survey rewards question, the corporate score on the rewards question dropped precipitously (four points), while cross-industry averages slowly rose. This was a highly significant change. In the behavioral sciences, "significant" means that the change did not happen by chance alone; something caused it to happen. Although the CHRO was not certain of the cause, he was certain about the solution: Push harder.

The next year, the CHRO announced that the corporation remained fully committed to becoming a high-performance organization and would further "strengthen" the process with a new rating-payout formula that would ensure that ratings would be tightly aligned with pay. The result? Another significant drop on the rewards score in both real terms and relative to a slowly rising cross-industry trend.

The third year, the CHRO reiterated the corporation's commitment to high performance and announced another tightening of the process by mandating expanded payout differences between high and low performers: High performers would get 20 percent salary increases, while mid to low performers would get none. The rewards score dropped another four points—again, a highly significant change. By the fourth year, just over one-third of all employees agreed that performance and rewards were linked. Employee perceptions of the performance-reward link shifted from five points above cross-industry averages to eight points below—a thirteen-point relative drop in just four years.

Like good politicians, the HR executive team celebrated the "success" of its new appraisal process. Since the company was one of the world's most respected HR organizations, the new "get tough" approach was heralded as a new standard in performance management and written up as a new best practice in numerous magazines, journal articles, and consulting pitches. There was no mention inside or outside the company that the actual result of the new process was a sharp drop in the belief that performance and rewards were linked. Programs, not results, mattered at this company and to the uncritical profession. No one ever asked, "Did it work?"

## What's Wrong with Today's Appraisals?

*"The Imperial Rater of Nine Grades seldom rates men according to their merits, but always according to his likes and dislikes."*

—FROM 3RD CENTURY WEI DYNASTY RECORDS

The scientific method is based on the Null Hypothesis. The Null Hypothesis presumes that a new theory, tool, or method is untrue unless evidence indicates otherwise. One cannot say, "The earth is flat. Prove me wrong." The guy who believes the earth is flat has to prove he's right. We all know that the appraisal cycle consumes vast amounts of time and energy, but few can show that their appraisal makes a difference. The burden of proof that it works must be on those who design and manage the process.

Before beginning an assessment of today's appraisal process, it is important to note that appraisals are neither inherently bad nor fatally flawed. They have potential to be a valuable and important part of an overall system for improving performance. Well-designed performance appraisals deliver three benefits to an organization:

1.  They focus employees on issues they can affect from their role and that are most important to business success.

2.  They maximize individual and collective team effort to achieve a challenging but attainable goal.

3.  They build employees' confidence and ability to make continual performance improvements.

Let's look at the reality of appraisals today, which are summarized in Table 7-2.

*Table 7-2. The need to realign performance appraisals.*

| TODAY'S MISGUIDED ASSUMPTIONS | CURRENT REALITY |
| --- | --- |
| Annual appraisals align the company | Appraisals often misalign the company |
| Appraisals are a rigorous method for assessing employee performance | Appraisal ratings are not perceived as valid |
| Forced distributions ensure fairness of pay decisions | Force distributions ensure demotivation and lack of cooperation |
| Appraisals strengthen manager-employee communication | Appraisals create manager-employee contention |
| Appraisals systematically improve average performance levels | Appraisals may systematically reduce performance levels |

**Problem #1: Appraisals Often Misalign the Company.** How likely is it that employees know in the first quarter which projects will be most important in the fourth quarter? For senior executives, annual metrics make sense; generally, the higher the organizational position, the longer the performance cycle.[2] For those in roles with shorter performance cycles, setting and adhering to an annual plan almost ensures misalignment with changing business needs. Dealing with this requires employees to set goals that are sufficiently ambiguous to deal with changes. Look back at Figure 3-6 in Chapter 3. It presents a good example of two HR executives who set intentionally ambiguous goals. How effectively do ambiguous goals drive performance? Not effectively at all.

**Problem #2: Appraisals Are Not Perceived as Valid.** I've always thought I could be a great race car driver. I enjoy speed and have good reaction time. However, the several times I paid to drive small race cars around a quarter-mile track (on Malibu Grand Prix courses), my times were no better than average. Trying a second or third time did not help, either. I just could not perform better than average. The data was clear: When it comes to racing, I do not have exceptional skills. I don't like this, but the feedback is fair and accurate and I accept it as a valid assessment of my driving skills. However, if a manager would have given me "feedback" on my driving skills, I would have been very resistant.

Table 7-1 showed that fairness and accuracy of feedback was found to be the most important of the 106 performance drivers studied by the Corporate Leadership Council. How often have you felt that your appraisal was truly fair and accurate? As mentioned earlier, almost nine out of ten employees believe that people in their organization do not receive the performance rating they deserve—and when it comes to motivation, perception is reality. If employees do not *believe* that appraisals are accurate, the appraisal process will not improve performance. Period.

This was the reason for the four-year drop in the perception of a performance-reward link in the case study of the Southeast Asian bank discussed earlier. Strengthening an appraisal process that is founded on ratings considered invalid by employees is like trying to put out a fire with gasoline. Put yourself in that position. You exit a performance review upset that your manager gave you a rating that seemed arbitrary and did not use information from people or data sources you see as relevant. The company uses that rating to rank you with peers who, you are convinced, are also not getting accurate ratings, which adds insult to injury. The company then widens payout differentials between those with high and low appraisal ratings. With each tightening turn, you become increasingly frustrated. What you really want is a fair and accurate rating that reflects a clear set of performance standards, and you want to be assessed by a manager who knows your performance firsthand and understands your work context. Look back at the "Top Drivers" in the first column of Table 7-1. That is what you want in an appraisal. Think of those as appraisal design principles.

**Problem #3: Forced Distributions Ensure Demotivation and Lack of Cooperation.** Forced ranking "discourages cooperation among workers and hurts productivity," according to a recent University of Michigan study.[3] "The use of rankings to scale employee performance relative to that of their peers, instead of using predetermined goals, may negatively affect employees' willingness to maximize joint gains that will benefit the organization," says Stephen Garcia, adjunct assistant professor of management and organizations at the University of Michigan's Ross School of Business, one of the authors of the study. Garcia's research found that when forced ranking is used, employees often care less about task performance and more about beating their colleagues. You know what that looks like: withholding information, backbiting, stealing credit. I can win if you lose. In many cases, forced ranking is a steroid for political gaming. And why would we want to do that?

Not only does forced ranking encourage organizational politics; it also reduces motivation and confidence. Many years of social psychology research has confirmed that when people compare themselves to peers, they evaluate themselves as above average. The effect is called the better-than-average effect. There are many studies and statistics on this, but basically speaking, the average performer rates him/herself as an 80th-percentile performer. For example, a study of college professors found that 94 percent considered their teaching ability to be above average.[4] This attribute is important for helping people maintain confidence and self-esteem. Would you tell your child that her abilities are just average or below average? If you do, your child will quickly move to that level (behavioral scientists call this the self-fulfilling prophecy). If you are a manager, your employees will do the same. This is what the third column ("Bottom Drivers") of Table 7-1 is all about.

If the average employee rates him/herself as an 80th-percentile performer and the average person is actually at the 50th percentile, appraisals ensure that most employees will be demotivated. On a typical five-point forced distribution scale, the top 10 percent will leave the review feeling good about themselves. The next 15 percent will leave with flat motivation or worse, 50 percent will be told they are average, and 25 percent—one out of four— will be told they are borderline or in serious trouble.[5] This doesn't sound like a success formula for improving workforce confidence and motivation.

Is the fix to tell everyone they are great? No, the fix is to reduce the tendency for individuals to make downward comparison choices and selectively recruit information that favors themselves. This can only happen when standards are clear and measured and when data does the talking—as in the Malibu Grand Prix example. Managers need to let the data show the individual where his/her performance stands and become the "personal trainer" to help the employee get stronger. More about that ahead.

**Problem #4: Appraisals Create Manager-Employee Contention.** A core manager responsibility is to motivate and develop. Good managers find daily opportunities throughout the year to motivate through praise, and by doing so, they continually raise confidence and raise the performance bar. Amos Alonzo Stagg, one of America's great football coaches, emphasized the role of "love" and doing what's best for each player rather than treating all the same. John Wooden, the most successful college basketball coach in U.S. history, also emphasized the importance of "love" when leading. He said that at the start of every season, he told his players, "I will love you all the same, but I won't like you all the same."[6] He went on to tell his players that what would appear to be a double standard was in reality working to get the most out of each person. Treating every person in the same way does not work as a parenting technique or a leadership tactic. Wooden goes on to say: "I made a genuine effort to connect with each player's life, his family, his classes and his interests. I was their leader, but we were a family and there was genuine love in my heart." Marcus Buckingham's finding that great managers manage employees differently puts hard data behind Wooden's thinking and what experienced parents know to be true—each person must be treated/lead differently.[7] Do you believe Wooden was able to extract full effort from his players even though did not offer them financial incentives?

Wooden motivated his players as a parent would motivate his/her children, with love and attention and praise. Make no mistake—failure to meet Wooden's high standards were met with an immediate rebuke, but it was done by a coach who was truly committed to the growth of his players.[8]

The reality of today's performance management system makes frequent praise problematic as it raises expectations at appraisal time. I still think about the time I was appointed to replace a terminated HR leader of a large business unit. When I began work, the existing HR staff were administrators and internal customer servants. My challenge was to shift these individuals into proactive, strategic partners who would be seen as key players for improving business performance.

We started the journey by building a business results–based HR strategy and scorecard with quarterly reviews. They were expected to shift from reacting to internal customer administrative requests to proactively improving business performance through people. For most, this required a 180° shift in thought and behavior.

I watched daily for activities and behaviors consistent with the new model, and I celebrated them every time. I was so proud of the dramatic shift in performance of each team member—and they knew it. HR performance metrics spiked in our first twelve months together; new behaviors delivered superb results that were acknowledged by the president and line managers, and through several best-in-class awards by national HR associations. Each of my direct reports was given an enthusiastic 1 rating by his/her business partner. They glowed with pride in their individual and our collective accomplishments. They had done what others in HR had only preached about. They were winners.

When appraisal time came around, I was only allowed to give one 1 rating. I needed to tell nine other people that their performance was just pretty good or worse. All of them were fully aware of their peers' accomplishments in other HR units in the company, and they knew they delivered far greater value to the business. In review after review, I broke the heart of each of these fine people. Each was convinced that he/she was a winner and believed I thought so too. They were right, but I had to meet my distribution requirements. My relationship with my direct reports changed that day from a warm, deeply caring one to a cold, business, professional one. Several subsequently left to apply their new skills in units that would "value their contributions."

**Problem #5: Appraisals May Systematically Reduce Performance Levels.** We talk teaming, but we appraise individuals. Not all jobs are team-centric, but many are. It is not rational for Joe to praise Jill, his peer, in front of others as Jill's perceived success will make Joe's own accomplishments shine less brightly. Think of Sara's performance appraisal from her parents at the beginning of this chapter. Why will she want to be a helpful big sister if she is being ranked against her siblings?

Having team members take part in hiring decisions is considered a staffing best practice. However, this practice is misaligned with the practice of forced ranking. Choosing outstanding candidates negatively affects the ratings and pay of current team members. And why would they want to be a good big brother/sister to a new hire? Similarly, why would a great employee want to transfer to a great team? And what about the problem I experienced (in the situation discussed above), where great team members move to weaker teams whose members they can outshine?

# Building a High-Performance Organization: The Roadmap

Building a high-performance organization requires a blueprint of success and an integrated system that delivers results to the blueprint. Creating individual programs around each of the Corporate Leadership Council's top seven performance drivers (from Table 7-1) will not deliver performance results. Performance results require a system. A system for building a high-performance organization, the good soil in which critical roles can thrive, requires excellence in three areas:

1. Strategy and alignment
2. Organizational culture
3. Appraisal and rewards

## Strategy and Alignment

When Lou Gerstner arrived at IBM in 1993, he visited general managers across the world and listened to many impressive strategic plans. Gerstner, a former director at McKinsey & Company, knew good strategy when he saw it, and much of what he saw was quite good. The problem was that good plans were not being executed at IBM, and customer and shareholder results continued to decline. At that time, IBM had been hiring top-tier general management firms to create business unit strategic plans. The firms spared no cost to make sure every number in the finished document was exact, no matter how small or insignificant. However, the answer to the question "Did IBM's strategic plans work?" was apparent in the company's near collapse. These strategy documents were very high-quality parts, but performance improvements required a strategic management system.

Gerstner's fix to the dilemma was for each business unit executive team to build a strategic management system by: (1) designing a differentiated strategy, (2) realigning the organization, and (3) cascading strategic objectives.

**Building the Strategy.** For more than a decade, IBM's business unit strategies have been created at the Strategic Leadership Forum at the Harvard Business School. This forum—a joint partnership between IBM and the Harvard Business School—is a three-and-a-half-day workshop attended by ten to fifteen executive team members of an IBM business unit where teams learn IBM's strategy model and vocabulary. They also spend seventeen hours in breakouts using those learnings to build a strategy and execution plan.

Teams prepare for the forum by reviewing large volumes of data on customers, financials, competitors, new technologies, etc. In addition, their staff members stay close to the phone throughout the forum to respond to requests for quick turnaround data. This data is not as polished as the general management firms might deliver, but it is good enough to determine a path. Most importantly, the forum allows team members to discuss, debate, and argue about the marketplace, customer needs and wants, and competitor moves. The Strategic Leadership Forum gets the entire leadership team on the same page with the same assumption sets. At the end of one-and-a-half days, the team has a statement of strategic intent, a common perspective on marketplace challenges, and a documented business model. Team discussions throughout the year are far more productive with this common assumption set.

What about lower-level leadership teams? Every leadership team needs a crystal-clear description—a blueprint—of success. If a CFO wants a world-class finance organization, what does that look like when it is complete and what are the steps to get there? A good book on setting direction is *The Power of Alignment* by George Labovitz and Victor Rosansky (John Wiley & Sons, 1997). The authors' process begins by defining the "main thing" an organization must accomplish. For FedEx, that is on-time overnight delivery. For a real estate agent, it is the breadth and depth of his/her community network. For a semiconductor organization, it is a full fabrication plan (FAB). Once the "main thing" is set, the organization chooses the three to six most important things to get right, each with a metric. The main thing to get right must be determined for each organizational unit.

**Creating Organizational Capabilities.** Any change in strategy requires a thoughtful assessment and realignment of the organization to the new strategy. There are many organizational alignment/capability models, but all are essentially the same. Choose one that is simple and easy to remember and use. I like the simplicity of the model in Figure 7-2. We used this model in Chapter 3 to realign HR to the new Human Capital Strategy. Any major change to a business strategy requires a similar diagnosis and realignment: All right-side boxes must explicitly align with the strategy, and each of the execution boxes must be integrated and aligned with each other box. For example, an acquisition strategy may require a dedicated team (structure), individuals with specialized skills in finding and buying companies (skills), detailed roadmaps for bringing the acquired company online (systems), and cultural integration to make sure employees in the acquired company do not leave (shared values).

*Figure 7-2. Organizational capabilities model.*

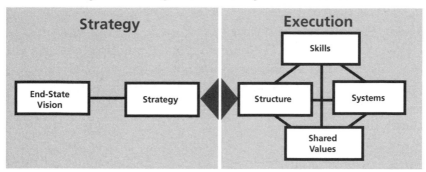

**Cascading Strategic Objectives.** Recently, I picked up my daughter from her first job at an upscale clothing retailer. I asked her, "Ashley, what is your role at the store? Do you sell clothes or stock shelves?" She said, "I don't know. I just do what they tell me to do." I continued, "Who are your store's target customers? Are they young, old, and what do they want from a clothing store?" She answered, "I don't know." I said, "Hmm, so what are the most important products to sell? What products does your company want you to push?" Again, her reply was, "I don't know. Nobody's told me."

It's pretty likely that the top executive team of this retailer held a multi-day strategy session where the business strategy was set. Soon after that, the marketing strategy would have been presented to the top team and elaborately described in the annual report. "This is it," the executive team members probably felt. "This is finally the plan that will truly set us apart!" The problem is that the only people who touch the customer are employees like my daughter, and she has no clue about the strategy.

This story is not unique. Accenture's 2004 High Performance Workforce study reported that only 20 percent of executives said three-fourths of their workforce understand the company's strategic goals.[9] What must an organization do to ensure that the work of people at the bottom of the organization is consistent with its strategy? What is the relative performance impact of doing that right versus conducting a good appraisal cycle?

When discussing the importance of organizational capabilities,

Fred Smith, chairman of FedEx, said, "One of the first things we recognized is that most managers don't know what management is about. Alignment is the essence of management."[10] Research by the Hay Group, the Gallup Organization, and organizations being published in many management journals suggests that the single most important thing to do for a manager to drive performance is to ensure that employees know what's expected of them. Great leaders create clarity and focus.

Seagate Technology is a 45,000-employee company that provides storage technology products and services. In 2001, Seagate executives felt that the company was wasting time and resources from overlapping and conflicting goals. The executives decided that a more rigorous and disciplined process would add significant business value. The process Seagate developed has two main components: (1) goal-setting and alignment workshops, and (2) an online goal-setting and management process.

Seagate's goal-setting workshops start with a top team session and work down. In the top team session, each member brings his/her goals to the meeting and places it on a Post-it Note underneath the larger strategic objectives. Breakout teams then examine and work through each goal for clarity and expected impact and ensure that each goal is fully integrated with other goals. These sessions force discussions around deeper assumptions and the full system required to deliver a business result. The sessions also create awareness of others' efforts and challenges. When all goals are sufficiently refined, alignment meetings are repeated with manager teams at the next level.

Goals are recorded on the company intranet for all to see. Each goal has an owner, a measure of success, and a due date. Any person who wants to know more about a particular goal can scroll up to identify the upward link or down to identify subgoals assigned to others.

Lenovo, an international technology company, has similar transparency. At Lenovo, any employee can look up the three top goals of any other employee. Such transparency improves goal quality and reduces the better-than-average-effect.

## Organizational Culture

Organizational culture is actually a part of the organizational model shown in Figure 7-2 (represented by "shared values"), but I would like to call it out for special attention. Culture, like strategy, is often viewed as an ephemeral construct. Most executives know it is important, but defining and measuring what "it" is remains unclear.

**What Is Culture?** Many executives give speeches on the importance of a high-performance culture, but few can precisely define what that culture is or how to arrive at that end-state. Culture change requires a clearly defined end-state, a team accountable for culture change, and ongoing disciplined measurement and management.

Culture is the sum of a set of shared values (see Figure 7-3). In day-to-day living, our values might include whether or when to get married, how many children to have, and expected educational achievements. At work, values might include innovation or personal growth. Values are composed of specific beliefs. For example, the value "personal growth" might comprise the following beliefs: "I believe that people should receive at least two weeks of formal training per year and that the role of managers is to help employees learn." If you want to change culture, change values. If you want to change values, change beliefs and behaviors.

*Figure 7-3. Culture, values, and beliefs.*

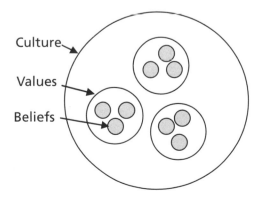

**Defining the Ideal Culture.** Many companies create generic value statements that offer little meaning or value to the organization. For instance, a European financial institution's values of (1) teamwork, (2) integrity, (3) respect, and (4) diversity were easy to remember, but they were relatively meaningless in driving business performance. All are important, for sure. However, these values might be more appropriately viewed as social values than as business values. Notice the difference in GE's values under Jack Welch: (1) boundarylessness, (2) intolerance of bureaucracy, and (3) reality-based conversations. These values were created to improve business performance.

Moving from a set of values to a defined set of behaviors is important. This feels a lot like the HCS principle of telling people "what to do" rather than "whom to be." When PriceWaterhouseCoopers Consulting was purchased by IBM in 2002, the integration team did just that. They created a values statement by soliciting input from many people. Once the values were finalized and the definitions attached, the team created scenarios to present good and bad behaviors. For example, teamwork is a good value, but it becomes more meaningful when scenarios are introduced. One such scenario goes like this: "The account manager is finalizing a solution sales to a client. To ensure that the client will buy, she reduces the software licensing fee. The software specialist is upset. What should you do?" The story then finishes with examples of good and bad teamwork. This presentation of scenarios shifts abstract values into concrete behaviors. As stated above, if you want to change culture, change values. If you want to change values, change beliefs and behaviors.

**Measuring the Culture.** Many companies today use standardized employee satisfaction/engagement surveys. They choose these because they are inexpensive, easy to use, and help the company compare itself with other companies inside and outside the industry. Although it is important to see how your company compares with competitors on generic engagement issues, it is also important to monitor progress to reach your defined culture.

It may be possible to accomplish both objectives of systematically improving the defined corporate culture and benchmarking with competitors on generic employee engagement items. Comparison against competitors can be assessed quarterly by surveying 3 to 5 percent of your employee base with the industry standard survey. However, because this data is drawn at a very high level, it will provide little if any understanding of root causes. Maybe training satisfaction was great in all units but one. With a small sample, you will not be able to know that. The quarterly survey is only about results to a given standard.

In addition, an annual full-employee survey defines the gap between the current and desired organizational culture. As much as possible, this data should be analyzed at the lowest work unit level. This depth enables survey leaders to search the data with the rigor of a finance professional who looks through results to find strong and weak spots by business unit and location. This depth also enables the top team to understand and teach other managers about the relationships between variables to make more informed human capital decisions.

**Managing the Culture.** Lou Gerstner understood the importance of a system in improving performance. He knew that IBM needed many large-scale change management initiatives. Change management theory suggests that ongoing leadership and support is essential. The problem was that with IBM on the brink of bankruptcy, there were too many initiatives that needed to be started and integrated to create one-off guiding coalitions. Creating coalitions for each change initiative would be too cumbersome and likely lead to uncoordinated change efforts. In response, Gerstner created the IBM Senior Leadership Team (SLT) of IBM's 300 best leaders. (Note that these are IBM's "best" leaders rather than the highest-ranking leaders.) At IBM, SLT members have two roles: (1) to serve as the standing coalition for change, and (2) to build leaders (the motto is, "leaders building leaders"). Continued membership on the SLT requires that members are role models for great leadership, drive organizational change, and actively build next-generation leaders. Every six months, IBM's chair personally makes, adds, and drops to the team based on each member's business performance and contribution to the team's mission. The SLT has created a powerful leadership culture in IBM.

The SLT concept is effective at lower organization levels as well. In 2001, IBM's ASEAN (Association of Southeast Asian Nations) region was struggling. The ASEAN region placed fifth of five Asia-Pacific regions in key IBM financial and customer measures. Satish Khatu, the new IBM ASEAN general manager, decided that organizational culture was one of the biggest problems. In response, he created a team called the ASEAN Leadership Team. Team membership was set at 100 and the IBM SLT rules of membership applied. The team's first task was to shift the IBM ASEAN culture to one of higher professionalism and accountability for results. Khatu made very clear behavioral statements of his expectations on these two dimensions.

Six months after the team began, Khatu dropped 20 percent of the team members as they either did not deliver to their assigned roles or they (and/or their group) did not demonstrate the new behaviors. That day, the culture made a sharp change. This was not the seven-year culture change often presented in change management books. That day, 100 of the most influential leaders of 10,000 ASEAN IBMers had to demonstrate a significant behavioral change, or there would be a heavy price to pay. To display the change, their direct reports also needed to demonstrate a similar shift of observable behaviors. With an average span of control of ten, (100 leaders × 10 direct reports = 1,000 people), the top 10 percent of all ASEAN IBMers, were immediately under the gun for demonstrable change.

The results of the culture change were dramatic. Within eighteen months, IBM ASEAN became IBM's #1 region in the world in sales to plan, #1 in profit to plan, and #1 in customer satisfaction. There were many reasons for those extraordinary business results, but the ASEAN Leadership Team—still in operation today—was a major contributor.

An SLT-type governance structure shifts human capital leadership tasks away from the top team to a cross-section of line leaders. It is a governance structure accountable for building a high-performance organization. Figure 7-4 presents an organizational arrangement where brand managers report hard or dotted line into the SLT. The other report line for key positions might go to the functional leader (e.g., product development or sales).

*Figure 7-4. Sample human capital governance model.*

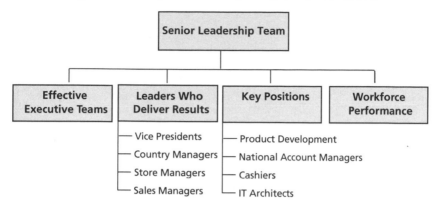

## Appraisal and Rewards

Early in my career as head of organization design at McDonald's, I asked a high-performing restaurant manager, "How do you reward your people?" He said, "Often, when we have a $1,200 lunch, I buy pizza and we celebrate." Later, I asked the same question of one of the top ten restaurant managers in the United States. He responded, "When we have a $1,200 lunch, I buy pizza and we celebrate." At first glance, their answers might seem the same, but look closely. With the addition of one significant word, these become two fundamentally different answers. In the first case, success is defined and rewards are provided at the discretion of a benevolent manager. In the second case, the bar is set, the performance contract is figuratively signed, and rewards come under the control of the team. A good manager sits in righteous judgment on his/her workers, while a great manager becomes a leader-servant who supports the crew to achieve its performance goals.

Let's take another example: real estate agents. Agents know the standard of success and the measures of performance. There is a small subjective component to the appraisal, to be sure: Agents who don't play fair with peers or agents in other offices must be corrected. But for the most part, agents evaluate themselves. Like crew members in the restaurant, real estate agents know precisely how they are performing to objective standards and how that performance compares to peers.

And like top McDonald's restaurant managers, real estate managers win when all agents are successful. In other words, they sit on the same side of the table as their agents.

But what if hard measures like sales volume are not possible? What about HR professionals or attorneys? Let's take an extreme example: Olympic platform divers. If valid judgments can be made here, they should be possible anywhere.

Diving assessments—scoring by the judges—may not be perfect but are pretty good. The assessments work for a few reasons. The first is that the performance standard (i.e., the standard for a perfect dive) is very clear. Point deductions are set for every deviation from that standard. Both judges and divers have a clearly defined picture of success.

The second reason the assessment works is that errors from subjective judgments are reduced with multiple raters. A basic law of statistics is that there is an inverse relationship between sample size and error—big samples cancel outliers (an observation that is distant from the rest of the data). Because of the clarity of performance standards used in diving, interrater reliability is generally close between judges, but there still is some variance as a result of human subjectivity. Diving assessments reduce this error by throwing out the top and bottom ratings and averaging the ratings of the other judges for a final score.

Google Corporation uses multiple raters at appraisal time to improve the validity and perception of fairness. At Google, employees and managers choose raters at the beginning of the appraisal cycle. These may include peers, cross-functional partners, and external customers. For jobs without hard financial or operational measures, Google uses subjective data and triangulates. At Google, this has improved the perception of fairness and accuracy of the performance appraisal process.

Finally, performance assessments in Olympic diving work well because of the "degree of difficulty" multiplier. This frees divers from having to perform identical dives. Each diver can be innovative and leverage his/her strengths, and each will stretch as far as possible to do something truly great. Contrast this with the sandbagging of goals that goes on each year in corporations. In 2007, Michael Jensen of The Monitor Group wrote a compelling article called "Paying People to Lie,"[11] where he asserts that our goal setting systems reward people for lying and punish them for telling the truth. He writes:

Tell a manager that he or she will get a bonus when targets are realized and two things are sure to happen. First, managers will attempt to set targets that are easily reachable, and once the targets are set, they will do their best to see that the targets are met even if it damages the company to do so.

How might adding the concept of degree of difficulty work in business? I recall a situation when I was a talent leader, and the two previous presidents of a joint venture in Korea had been terminated in the last four years. It looked as though we had had an "impossible job"—a job that was structured in a way that failure was inevitable. A third president came in and managed to hold on. He didn't post any big numbers, but he held the company together and kept it on a steady performance track. Given the degree of difficulty, we rated his performance a 1.

What principles can we extract from the McDonald's, real estate agent, and Olympic diving performance management models?

- *Let's make a deal.* Set the bar and empower. This standard is absolute, not relative.

- *Manager as coach, not judge.* The manager is rewarded for all 1 ratings of his/her workers. Employee failure is a management failure.

- *Real-time feedback.* Immediate feedback improves performance.

**Let's Make a Deal.** Many HR generalists have confronted angry sales reps who exceeded quotas but received ratings of "meets expectations" or "below expectations" as a result of a forced ranking system. "How can you tell me I performed below expectations when I was at 113 percent of quota?" a sales rep in such a situation would say. It's pretty difficult to explain that the forced distribution policy requires that a certain percentage of employees be rated below expectations regardless of whether or not they actually did meet expectations. One way to address the problem is to say something like, "Of course you exceeded expectations, but I only have so many 1 and 2 ratings to give." Another way is to obscure performance measures so no one really knows whether the person made it or not. This reduces the chance that the manager will be called a hypocrite, but it also compromises two powerful performance drivers: understanding performance standards, and fairness and accuracy of feedback.

As in the McDonald's example above, performance management methods that improve performance require an unambiguous bar and a clear deal between managers and employees. But what if the company insists on forced ranking? No problem: Just make sure that this is the deal managers and employees strike at the beginning of the year. Let's take a sales example. The manager says, "Sue, your performance rating will be based on your quota attainment relative to your other national account managers in the Western Region. If you hit 120 percent of quota and the average NAM hits 125 percent, you will receive a below average performance rating." In a business that requires teamwork between reps, count on this to be problematic. In one where employees do not regularly interact, it may work well. In any case, it is important to measure whether it works or not. For example, ask the following questions:

- What was the change in sales revenue?
- What happened with NAM turnover?
- What were the performance characteristics of the NAMs who left?
- What happened to the corporate culture?

That is not to imply that results-only is the best model. It is not. In roles with objectively measured outputs such as manufacturing, call centers, and sales, business results often overshadow softer issues. Alternatively, in support functions such as human resources and communications, softer measures such as contribution to the professional community overshadow hard results. That's not so good either. We have discussed hard results, so now let's look at the softer side. (Caution is required when wandering into the soft side, since this is where most appraisals come off-track.)

One sure way to knock appraisals off-track is to appraise competencies. As mentioned earlier in Chapter 5, competencies may be good predictors of performance in an employee's next job, but the best measure of performance in the current job is . . . performance. If you can deliver to the negotiated performance standards while scoring below average on the competency "personal dedication," maybe personal dedication was not needed for your job, or maybe your boss assessed it wrong. In either case, this is a past-oriented performance appraisal, not a future-oriented competency assessment. You and your boss made a deal.

A better subjective component is the extent to which the individual strengthened the desired culture. With cultural definitions like teamwork and diversity, such an assessment is difficult. It would be ideal if your company had a clearly defined culture, but the reality is that few companies do. If the company does not have a good set of values and desired behaviors, then the manager should set his/her own.

PepsiCo uses both performance and behaviors when rating managers. PepsiCo's research found that of employees who intended to stay with the company, 94 percent were satisfied with their manager. For those who intended to leave, only 42 percent were satisfied with their manager.[12] Yet PepsiCo was not systematically increasing the number of employees satisfied with their manager. The executive team felt a single rating mix of performance and leadership weighed too heavily on performance.

PepsiCo's fix was to create a dual performance rating system where managers receive separate performance and leadership ratings. The corporation extended this to almost all employees as dual ratings for business results and people results—another way of measuring personal impact on organizational culture. Each rating is weighted for a final rating that is used for compensation decisions. For managers, performance results are weighted at .66 and leadership results are weighted at .34. You are probably wondering whether more employees were now satisfied with their manager. The rating on PepsiCo's employee survey that managers are held accountable for both business results and people results improved by 6 percentage points, but in a twenty-two-page report on the dual rating system, the question about manager satisfaction improvements was not addressed. What does that tell us about the emphasis on results versus programs?

Another way to assess subjective performance is by using key results. Remember the NAM example in Chapter 6, where the company needed to shift from a product to a solution sale? If quota was the only success measure, few would venture into the unknown world of solution selling. One way to fix this is to set quotas separately for products and for solutions. Another way is to define and measure selling solutions behavior.

Finally, what deal has your company made with its employees on base and bonus payouts? I once asked an executive, "What is your bonus based on?" "Performance," he said. "I see," I said, "then what's your salary increase based on?" "Performance," he answered. "What's the difference?" I asked. He shrugged. What about your company? What deal have you made with your employees?

Consider this: Base pay increases are a function of value to the company and inflation; incentives are awarded for in-year performance results. A sales rep can get lucky or unlucky in any given year. A key account has a great year or goes bankrupt. In both cases, performance is paid out in an incentive check. Sometimes you get lucky and sometimes you don't; that is the nature of sales. However, this should not result in career-long annuities. When you hire a new employee, you set his/her salary based on the expected value to the business. That philosophy should be continued during employment. Value to the company may be assessed by three-year performance averages, the possession of a highly valued and rare skill, the ability to deliver game-changing performance breakthroughs, etc. Base pay for value to the business; bonus for in-year results.

## Manager as Coach, Not Judge

When the bar is set and the deal is made, the manager can move from across the table as judge to the same side of the table as coach. The star McDonald's restaurant manager, the real estate manager, and the Olympic diving coach want nothing less for each individual than to take first place. Valid, objective performance measures enable managers to give as much positive feedback as they feel is optimal. If key results are well-designed, these will be the focal points for improving the performance of each employee. An organization's best managers will grow their employees faster on each key result than its average managers. Year-over-year change on key results is an important metric for assessing manager performance.

## Real-Time Feedback

The very best way for managers to improve employee performance is to set clear expectations and hold regular business reviews to those expectations. One hundred years of research in learning has shown the importance of immediate feedback for performance improvement of humans, rats, and bugs. It should be no surprise that real-time feedback drives performance at work and that an annual performance appraisal does little for performance improvements.

It has been my consistent experience that the very best managers almost always have a series of regular reviews that balance leading and lagging indicators and serve less as judgment sessions and more as coaching sessions. Want better performance? Hold monthly reviews. Immediate feedback from these reviews is far more likely to improve performance than a single review in December. The most powerful performance improvement levers—fairness and accuracy of feedback, understanding performance standards, internal communication, and the manager being knowledgeable about performance—are all outcomes of regular monthly reviews. Employees who see reviews as coaching sessions and feel that their manager sits on the same side of the table enthusiastically attend and are more open to both negative and positive feedback.

# Conclusion

The preceding chapters of this book have focused on improving the performance of those in critical roles. Think of these as seeds. Good seeds require good soil. In this case, that soil is a high-performance organization. Exactly what is a high-performance organization?

When most people talk about performance improvements, they focus on training and appraisals, but training and appraisals are parts of an engine—not the engine itself. Parts cannot make an engine run. An engine needs a system of integrated parts. This is why data indicates that neither training nor appraisals have a significant impact on employee performance. Improving performance through a high-performance organization requires a blueprint of the engine—a completed architectural drawing and a roadmap for getting to there from here.

A high performance organization requires:

- Strategy and alignment
- Organizational culture
- Appraisal and rewards

Defining the main thing to get right is the first step. For the corporation or business units, this might be expressed in terms of a strategy. For departments, this might be expressed as the purpose or the main things to get right. For HR departments using the new Human Capital Strategy, there are two things to get right: (1) to ensure that the organization can deliver its annual business plan, and (2) to continually improve performance of those in critical roles. Job descriptions, job evaluations, incentive and benefit programs, and the like must align with one of those two objectives. The main thing starts from the top and works down.

The next step is to ensure that the organization is capable of delivering the strategy or main thing. For example, is it structured correctly? Do you have the right number of people and skills? The goals must be deliberately cascaded to ensure that all those who work in the organization are working on issues that are critical to the business and to accomplishing the main thing of the unit.

The third step is to ensure that the culture supports the strategy or main thing. The culture defines what gets rewarded. An HR department that embarks on the Human Capital Strategy must make sure that results and not likeability is rewarded.

The fourth step is to create an appraisal and reward system that aligns with the strategy, cascaded goals, and desired culture. The appraisal system is the glue that brings it all together and holds it in place. The design principles for appraisals that improve performance are:

- *Let's make a deal.* Set the bar and empower. This standard is absolute, not relative.
- *Manager as coach, not judge.* The manager is rewarded for all 1 ratings of his/her workers. Employee failure is a management failure.
- *Real-time feedback.* Immediate feedback improves performance.

Making a deal means setting the bar and making a deal between manager and employee of the consequences of making or missing the objective. However, if your organization is set on forcing performance to a normal curve, then managers must make that assumption clear when making the deal. The manager must say, "Performance will be relative, not absolute. You must outperform your peers."

A clear deal between manager and employee enables the manager to move from across the table as judge to side-by-side as coach and supporter. It also frees the manager to provide positive feedback without worrying that positive feedback during the year will create an expectation of a high rating at year-end.

The better-than-average effect states that the average person sees him/herself as better than average. This effect can be reduced by providing employees with real data about peers. Transparency states that everyone should know everyone else's goals and performance to the goals. Today's online capabilities make this an easy task.

Finally, an effective performance management system requires real-time feedback. Business reviews are an ideal way to keep employees and managers focused and accountable all year long. Pushing harder is not always a bad thing. Maintaining that steady push all year long will certainly deliver better annual results.

# Notes

1. Accenture, *High Performance Workforce Study* (2004), p. 8. Accessed on www.accenture.com (April 6, 2007).

2. E. Jacques, "Taking Time Seriously in Evaluating Jobs," *Harvard Business Review* (September–October 1979).

3. "Forced Rankings of Employees Bad for Business," University of Michigan Ross School, http://www.bus.umich.edu/newsroom/articledisplay.asp?news_id=9730. (Accessed on April 24, 2007.)

4. P. Cross, "Not can, but will college teachers be improved?" *New Directions for Higher Education*, Volume 17 (1977), pp. 1–15.

5. Corporate Leadership Council, *Forced Ranking Systems in Relation to Salary Administration* (Washington, D.C.: Corporate Executive Board, 2001).

6. J. Wooden and J. Carty, *Coach Wooden: One-on-One* (Ventura, Calif.: Regal Books, 2003), Day 30.

7. M. Buckingham and C. Coffman, *First, Break All the Rules* (New York: Simon & Schuster, 1999).

8. J. Wooden and S. Jamison, *The Essential Wooden: A Lifetime of Lessons in Leaders and Leadership* (New York: McGraw-Hill, 2007).

9. Accenture, p. 6.

10. G. Labovitz and V. Rosansky, *The Power of Alignment* (Hoboken., N.J.: John Wiley & Sons, 1997), p. 6.

11. M. Jensen, "Paying People to Lie," http://www.monitor.com/cgi-bin/iowa/ideas/index.html?article=121. Accessed on May 31, 2007.

12. Corporate Leadership Council (2005). *PepsiCo's Dual Performance Rating Practice: An Overview of the Practice and a Conversation with Allan Church, Vice President of Organization and Management Development.* Washington, D.C., Corporate Executive Board.

# Chapter Eight

# Putting It All Together

*"A leader is someone who steps back from the entire system and tries to build a more collaborative, more innovative system that will work over the long term."*

—ROBERT REICH

The purpose of this last chapter is to create a roadmap for building and executing the new Human Capital Strategy. Here again, let's use the Human Capital Management model as a generic roadmap (see Figure 8-1). Certainly, every organization is unique and will choose a different path depending on circumstances. This chapter is one way to proceed; it may or may not be the right way for your organization. The chapter is written with a stand-alone unit—a company, business unit, or geographic organization (e.g., region, country)—in mind. Given space constraints, it is not possible to provide detailed work plans, meeting agendas, data collection tools, internal communications templates, etc.

Figure 8-1. The Human Capital Management model.

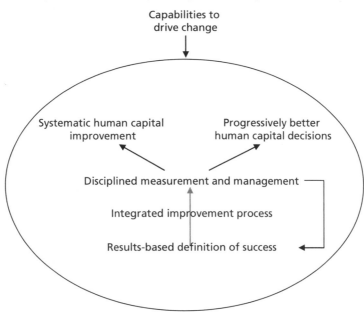

# Step 1: Create Capabilities to Drive Change

As emphasized in the preceding chapters, the first step in the journey is to build organizational capabilities to lead the change. Designing and executing an HCS requires three distinct senior manager roles, which are presented in Table 8-1. Note that unique responsibilities are assigned for individuals in each role, and each must clearly understand his/her duties. However, more importantly, each senior leadership member accepts full responsibility for organization-wide human capital excellence. This is no different from sports team members playing different positions. Each is individually responsible for position excellence and jointly responsible with teammates for a team win. Shared accountability by top team members may be *the* most important of all critical success factors for human capital improvement.

## General Manager

Systematic human capital growth requires general managers to elevate the importance of human capital to the level of financial and customer

Table 8-1. *Primary Human Capital Strategy roles.*

| ROLE | ACCOUNTABLE PERSON/TEAM | PRIMARY ACCOUNTABILITY |
|---|---|---|
| HCS owner | General manager | Manage to a balance scorecard—insist on results, select SLT members, and run the SLT |
| Day-to-day HCS leader | Top HR leader for the unit | Content expert, project manager, tactical organization-wide change leader |
| Governance body | Senior Leadership Team | Adviser to top HR leader, role model; uses influence and resources to enable HR leader to leverage organization members to deliver results |

results. Past and current inabilities of organizations to systematically improve human capital is largely because few GMs manage human capital with the same discipline as financial capital. They do not insist on year-over-year performance improvements from their line executives or from their HR function.

Shifting to a balanced management approach begins with a balanced scorecard. Some organizations use a balanced scorecard today, but how many manage their business in a balanced way? I have been in many senior management meetings where monthly revenue and profit discussions consume 95 percent or more of the team's time. Customer and employee issues are addressed at the very end, when the team is tired and some are packing up to catch a flight home. Time after time, top team members leave, frustrated that they shortchanged people issues.

But the problem extends beyond meetings and into day-to-day behavior. Look at the annual objectives and monthly calendars of top team members. What is important? When the GM is waiting for an elevator and meets some direct reports, what questions does he/she ask? Success is a balanced approach to daily business management, not simply the presence of a balanced scorecard.

Monthly/quarterly human capital reviews are a good place to begin a cultural shift to balanced management. You may choose to integrate human capital reviews into existing business reviews or conduct the reviews as stand-alone meetings. In either case, decide who will attend and what specific questions you will ask at each review. This creates focus, similar to a school test where the student knows the questions well before the test.

## Senior Leadership Team

An ongoing Senior Leadership Team is the second human capital role. As discussed in Chapter 7, an SLT can be an effective governance body for improving organizational capabilities. The SLT assumes the primary leadership role for long-term capability improvements by serving in the capacity of a board of directors for human capital growth and organizational change. Its core duty is to ensure that the organization learns from experience and continually improves its ability to grow its human capital and effectively manage change. See Table 8-2 presents the responsibilities and rewards of SLT members.

In many organizations today, program designers must sell their program stakeholder by stakeholder across the organization. Let's take a new talent management system, for example. The program designer must get buy-in from a set of influential HR leaders, line leaders, and top team members. This can be an excruciatingly slow process of one-on-one meetings where any one person can stop or redirect the new initiative. Often, designers struggle to appease stakeholders who insist on "going left" while at the same time appeasing those who insist on "going right." The resulting compromise produces a program or system that meets most or all needs but is unable to produce the intended result.

An SLT shortchanges this process. At an SLT meeting, the same talent management program designer might spend thirty minutes pre-

*Table 8-2. SLT members' responsibilities and rewards.*

| WHAT SLT MEMBERS GIVE | WHAT SLT MEMBERS GET |
|---|---|
| 1–2 days per quarter to improve HCS results | Respect and recognition for being considered the best of the best |
| Role model behavior—adherence to desired culture | 75th percentile pay and options |
| Individual business performance excellence | Focused coaching and development |

senting the project to the team, after which team members engage in a spirited discussion for about sixty minutes. When time is up, a decision is made, and when the SLT makes its decision, every member must support that decision or risk being dropped from the SLT. Criteria for approval/modifications include: (1) fit with, and impact on, the business and human capital strategies; (2) synergy with other projects underway; and (3) ability to measure performance outputs. SLT members return to their offices with a deep understanding of what changes are coming, why each change is needed, the root cause, the critical success factors for ensuring that good plans become good results, and their own role in ensuring initiative success.

Creating an SLT requires the GM to choose 2 to 10 percent of the organization's best leaders as team members. It is critically important that members are not selected by management level but by leadership excellence; in other words, membership is earned. Choosing the less controversial approach where membership is an entitlement would reduce an SLT's effectiveness. Some members would attend meetings, while others would not. Some would support team initiatives and role model expected behavior, while others would not.

Make sure the criteria for SLT membership is clear. Consider the following: (1) individual business performance, (2) contribution to SLT results, (3) role modeling the desired culture, and (4) track record of developing great leaders. Every six months, the GM reviews performance of every SLT member on each criterion. Those who fall below a defined threshold are dropped and others are added to fill openings. The concept of an SLT is founded on a well-researched principle that proportionally higher investments in top performers yields better rates of return than equally distributed investments or investments in underperformers.

Getting the right members on the SLT is an important first step. The next and equally important step is to hold effective SLT meetings. These meetings should not be formal decision forums for approving backroom deals. Rather, SLT meetings are working sessions for surfacing truth. I do not know of a good English term for surfacing truth through a challenging discussion. The Japanese term is *giron*—the intersection of dialogue/debate/discussion. When a *giron* is called in Japan, formality is put aside and the team pursues a quest for truth. (An article on how to create an effective *giron* is "How Management Teams Can Have a Good Fight," *Harvard Business Review*, July 1997.)

## Top HR Leader

The top HR leader assumes the role of day-to-day leader for organizational and human capital improvements. This role goes far beyond today's ideal of being a business partner who sits at the right tables and offers sage advice. As the organization's change leader (versus a leader of people-related programs), the top HR professional must deliver real value to the organization.

It is unfair to members of the HR function to demand a flash cut change to a change leadership role. Making this transition requires time. Unfortunately, many HR departments have asked for more time for decades now and yet made little progress. This time, things have to be different.

A system for shifting HR professionals to organizational change leaders begins by resetting HR's model to conform to the recommendations presented in Chapter 3. First, focus on *structure*. Create fully separate HR administration and HCM organizations. Assign HR professionals either to administrative or HCM roles, but do not allow individuals to hold accountabilities for both. Doing so almost guarantees that HR professionals will say that they cannot do value-added work because they are too busy fighting fires. The old will almost certainly strangle the new.

The second system component is measurement *systems*. Separate budgets and performance measures for administrative HR and HCM organizations. Define HR administrative success as cost efficiency and legal compliance. Define HCM success as fully executing the HCS and annual business plans. Keep these measurement systems and budgets separate.

The third system component is change management *skills*. Hire full-time organization effectiveness (OE) professionals.* OE professionals

---

*OE professionals are also called Organization Development (OD) professionals, change management experts, and sometimes even organization designers. Different terms, but they do the same work.

often sort into two types: (1) the kind who operate like mechanics, searching for root causes and building systems for improvement; and (2) the kind who operate like social workers/psychiatrists, seeing organizational change as an individual process that requires team members to surface and discuss feelings. My experience suggests that among OE professionals, one-third are mechanics and two-thirds are social workers. Each group works off a different human capital theory. Know which you want and be vigilant when hiring. Consider hiring independent consultants on long-term contracts (good OE professionals—especially mechanics—are in very short supply). The goal is to have the skills present; it may not matter whether these are contract or full-time employees.

Finally, the fourth system component to change are the *shared values*, or the culture of HR. Start by examining the annual performance goals for the HR leaders and their direct reports. Are performance goals activity-based or results-based? If customers or shareholders read the goals, would they care? Start the behavior change by inspecting every HR professional's annual goals. Then schedule quarterly reviews in advance of line executive reviews to examine the progress on each performance objective. Ensure that every HR professional makes quarterly commitments of what he/she will deliver within the twelve-week time period to improve customer and shareholder satisfaction. At the end of the twelve weeks, the HR professional should say, "Here is the Power-Point slide I used at the start of the quarter to make my commitments. This is what I said I would do, and here is what I did." Then, the HR professional would say, "Here is what I will do next quarter to improve customer and shareholder satisfaction and advance the HCS." These reviews provide an opportunity to adjust annual goals to ensure that the HR professional is working on the most important activities.

Employee turnover of OE professionals is much higher than turnover among HR generalists. Many good OE professionals quit corporate roles to become independent consultants—not for the money, but to flee the constant tension between being a loyal HR community member and doing the right thing for their business partners. Continually ask the OE professionals if they experience tension between the two constituency groups. Use these folks as your "canary in the bird cage" for sensing changes in the HR culture.

*Table 8-3. Checklist for HCS*
*organizational capabilities.*

1. Does the GM and top team use a balanced scorecard?
2. Do they use a balanced approach to managing the business?
3. Are HCS monthly reviews set for the year? Is the agenda, attendees, etc., fixed?
4. Is the SLT membership criteria and reassessment schedule set?
5. Have SLT members been chosen?
6. Has the SLT finalized its charter and operating guidelines?
7. Has the unit's top HR leader committed to be the organization's change leader?
8. Is the HR structure aligned to deliver business results?
9. Are administrative and strategic HR roles separate?
10. Are individual performance goals aligned to the HCS and annual business objectives?
11. Does HR have access to industry-best change management skills?
12. Is there a disciplined approach with measurable milestones for improvement in change management skills?

Table 8-3 is a checklist for ensuring that organizational capabilities exist in your company.

# Step 2: Define Success

Step 1 was about creating organizational capabilities to lead change. If no one is in charge of human capital growth, no progress is possible. A major reason that good books, articles, and best practices fail to take root is that human capital ownership and management falls between organizational silos. Remember the advice in the book *Good to Great*: First, get the right people on the bus. Then put the people in the right seats. Then determine where the bus will go. Only after the organization is fully readied to drive change should an HCS be designed.

Defining success—how we will know we've arrived—and creating a strategy for getting there is the role of the SLT. The tasks below provide a roadmap for defining success and creating a strategy to get there. Consider addressing each step below at the first SLT meeting. Before the meeting, ask members to review Chapter 2 of this book (outlining the Human Capital Strategy), or summarize it for them to jumpstart the process.

## Set the Human Capital Theory and Lagging Indicator

Start by defining your organization's human capital theory—how people contribute to performance excellence. Is success defined as fairness and equity, lawsuit prevention, employee self-actualization, critical role excellence, employer-of-choice status, or something else? Gaining agreement here is important as it provides a foundation for all other human capital decisions.

Once the theory is clear, define the ultimate measure—the grand lagging indicator that will measure whether the organization has succeeded. If the human capital theory stresses the importance of fairness and equity, the lagging indicator may be the results of a customized employee satisfaction questionnaire. If it is to be the employer of choice, then it might be the results of a survey of professionals across your industry. If it is workforce performance, consider the Profit per Employee metric discussed in Chapter 2.

## Set the Human Capital Strategy

Once the human capital theory and lagging indicators are documented, create your company's Human Capital Strategy. Do this at the first SLT meeting after the theory is complete, maybe in late morning or early afternoon. Again, having members read Chapter 2 of this book ahead of time is helpful in getting them on the same page.

Post the assumptions from the pre-read, conduct a *giron* around each, document the discussion outcome, and read it back to the SLT for formal approval. For example, you might wish to reach agreement on the following:

- Do we believe that the purpose of performance management is to improve performance?

- Do we agree that human capital success should be gauged by performance rather than by program quality?

- Will we accept the assertion that a leadership culture is the most important CSF for leadership performance improvements?

## THE STRATEGIC PARTNER VS. THE FACILITATOR

Many organization effectiveness consultants and HR leaders choose a facilitative role during strategy development. These professionals are often of the opinion that smart executives will create a good plan. It is my consistent experience that this is an incorrect assumption. Would one expect the same group of smart SLT members to independently create a highly effective IT system? Probably not, since content expertise is required. Intelligence is a necessary but not sufficient condition for making good human capital decisions.

Too often, in a purely facilitative approach, team members address symptoms and craft solutions to the symptoms. Instead, use a content expert to steer the discussion to enable smart people to make smart decisions. Find a facilitator who is capable of *leading* a discussion that emerges with a plan that delivers real results. A good question to ask throughout the discussion is: "On a 1 to 100 scale, how likely is it that this plan will be fully executed and deliver the desired results?"

The purpose of an HCS is to systematically strengthen an organization's sustained competitive advantage. Make sure your HCS does this. Think of the HCS as the architect's blueprint: what it looks like when you have succeeded. Define the phases, milestones, and key dates that tell all organizational employees that progress is being made. Use a construction metaphor: when will the foundation be complete, at what date will the walls be raised, etc. Put milestone announcement dates on the calendar and share the calendar with all employees. Publicly make and meet HCS commitments.

Table 8-4 provides a checklist for ensuring a solid strategy.

*Table 8-4. Checklist ensuring a solid human capital strategy.*

1. Is there SLT consensus around the human capital theory?
2. Have you chosen a lagging indicator?
3. Are HCS assumptions documented?
4. Will the resulting HCS deliver the lagging indicator?
5. How and when will HCS progress be measured?
6. Is the HCS sufficiently simple for all employees to understand?
7. Are employees aware of the phases and milestone dates?

# Step 3: Create an Integrated Improvement Process

An integrated improvement process starts at the top with the business strategy and works down. Let's break the integrated improvement process into two stages:

1. Align all activities to a business strategy.
2. Improve performance of those in critical roles.

## Align All Activities to a Business Strategy

The first task is to ensure that leadership teams, from the top down, can simply describe the business strategy. To check, stop ten employees in the hallway and ask:

- What are the three to five most important things our company needs to accomplish this year?
- Is there a strong reason for customers to buy from us rather than our competitors?
- How are customer needs changing? How are competitors changing?
- How will our company change over the next three years?

If members of the top team cannot answer the questions consistently, there may be no strategy. If they can, but those at lower organizational levels cannot, there may be a communications and alignment issue. Asking these four questions to top team members and also to individuals at lower levels will help you understand the current state.

The process of building a business strategy is outside the scope of this book. Let's work here with the assumption that there is such a business strategy; in many organizations, that is the case. However, in the large majority of organizations where I have served, the strategy is unclear, even to top team members, and misaligned with the multitude of daily decisions by those at all organizational levels. An excellent strategy unknown by organization members will deliver little value to customers and shareholders.

**Clarify the Business Strategy.** An executable strategy requires distilling lots of thinking and analysis down to a set of four to six strategic objectives. Strategic objectives (SOs) are the things the business must deliver to achieve its short- and mid-term financial expectations. Examples include acquiring a company, creating a new service offering, and strengthening partnerships. SOs can be an effective tool when top team members give consistent answers to the following questions:

- Given our strategy, what are the four to six results that matter most to customers and shareholders?
- Who is the lead and who is the support for each strategic objective?
- How and when will we measure the performance of each?
- What are the three most important things I must do to fully execute these plans?

Once SOs are in good shape, the next task is to define critical success factors—the five to seven internal things to get right to deliver the strategic objectives. As mentioned earlier, CSFs are the necessary and sufficient conditions for success.[1] These may include financial controls, cost reductions, etc. Unlike SOs, customers do not care about CSFs. You will know your CSFs are in good shape when top team members give consistent answers to the following questions:

- What are the five to seven CSFs that are the most important things to achieve the strategic objectives?
- Who owns each CSF?
- What is our management method for ensuring CSF improvements?

---

### ASSIGNING CSG OWNERSHIP

A common error when setting CSFs is for the GM to accept ownership for one or more CSFs. The GM is the owner of all, but the day-to-day leader of none. CSFs must be unambiguously assigned to a given team member. The situation where someone can say, "We both kind of own that CSF" rarely works. The role of the assigned executive team leader is to ensure progress on the portfolio of CSF projects.

---

**Redesign the Organization.** This next step is also outside of the scope of this book, but it is critically important. It is to ensure that the business is properly organized to deliver the SOs. This may require macro-organizational adjustments such as moving from vertically aligned functions (e.g., purchasing, logistics, and billing) to process-aligned units (e.g., supply chain organization). It might also require more micro-level changes such as permanent cross-profession design teams. Organizational design is one of the most powerful tools for creating performance improvements, but also one of the most difficult and disruptive.

**Cascade Strategic Objectives and Critical Success Factors.** Once the direction from the top is clear and the organization is realigned to the new strategy, the next step is to cascade goals from the top to the bottom of the organizational hierarchy. Getting all organization members to row the boat in the same direction is a valuable short-term lever for improving productivity and performance. Remember Fred Smith's admonition (discussed in Chapter 7) that "Alignment is the essence of management?" Goal setting, monthly/quarterly business reviews, appraisals, and compensation plans are tools/programs for strengthening organizational alignment and focus.

In many organizations today, goal cascades are part of the annual performance management cycle, but how well do these cascades work? If each member achieves his/her annual performance goals, will the organization absolutely achieve its strategic objectives? Probably not. More often than not, individual performance goals are set by the manager's request to "Make sure your goals are aligned with mine." Sounds a lot like the "Hope Strategy"—let's do something and hope it works.

A more disciplined approach to alignment explicitly links all organization members with the business's strategic objectives and/or CSFs. This begins by carefully aligning all top team objectives with each SO and CSF. The next step is to work with "next level down" leadership teams to help set their objectives. For example, if CSF #3 is "grow brand awareness," that may become the "main thing" for the marketing department. The marketing group then set its four to six CSFs required to grow brand awareness. The cascade continues on down. A disciplined cascade looks like the example in Figure 8-2.

*Figure 8-2. An example of a disciplined goal cascade.*

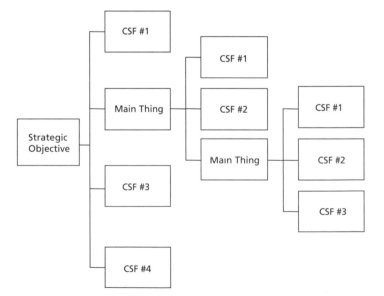

**Set the Organizational Culture.** It is the responsibility of the SLT to make sure your "to-be" organizational culture—the desired culture—is commonly understood and progress is being made on organizational capability issues. Too many organizations use single words to describe company values. For example, a common value is "respect." What "respect" means varies by individual. Violation of this corporate value is often challenged when layoffs are announced. What "respect" actually is and how it ties to the organization's vision and strategy is unclear. Look at Goldman Sachs's website as a contrast (www2.goldmansachs.com). It lists twelve very clear business principles that define the culture. A similar document is the first step in creating real culture change in your organization.

Once the "to-be" culture is documented, the SLT must use objective measures for each culture dimension to define current gaps and to create gap closure plans. Assign an SLT owner/team to build a rigorous gap closure plan with milestones and public read-out dates.

## Improve Performance of Those in Critical Roles

An integrated improvement process begins by ensuring that organizational members are aligned to a common strategy and rowing in the same direction. The next task is to systematically improve the performance of those in critical roles. Success is being able to answer the following questions:

- Do those in critical roles outperform competitor peers?
- Does your system improve critical role performance year-over-year?

**Identify Critical Roles.** It is not possible to have an effective organization without an effective executive team. Even small executive team decisions can create huge amounts of work and distraction below. In almost every organization, the executive team is a critical role and, as such, should be measured and managed as other critical roles.

Other critical roles depend on your business and its strategy. Will your organization choose to focus on specific positions (such as country general manager or sales manager) or by organization level (vice presidents, directors, etc.)? Whichever you choose, the output will be a list of roles. Improving year-over-year performance of those in critical roles will create value for customers and shareholders.

**Define Performance Results for Each Critical Role.** For each role, define the four to six most important performance results and assess every community member on each. Build a database of all community members and populate the database with the assessment results (see Table 5-4 in Chapter 5 for an example). Then realign all HR systems so that each is optimally effective for driving performance improvement on each of the four to six results. For example, if a performance result for region managers is "high-performance culture," review all HR systems to ensure that they support the result:

- Is culture change training offered?
- Do annual performance objectives include culture?
- Do appraisals include a component for role modeling the culture?
- Are new managers selected by their track record for culture change?
- Do compensation incentives support culture change?

**Create Governance Structure for Each Role.** Accountability must be unambiguously assigned for driving year-over-year performance improvements of those in critical roles. For positions with scale—say, 100 or more incumbents—consider a knowledge community or brand manager–type approach as described in Chapter 6. In this approach, a single person from the community is selected to provide day-to-day leadership for community performance improvements.

The community leader starts by creating a community dialogue around each lagging indicator of performance, then creates a system for improving performance on this indicator. Let's look again at the example of knowledge community system components, shown in Figure 8-3 (which was first presented in Chapter 6).

Figure 8-3. Knowledge community system components.

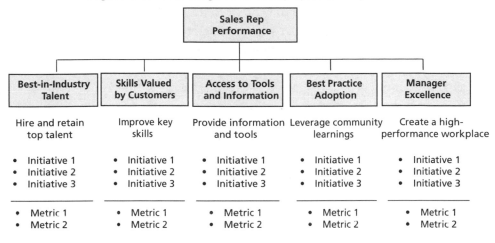

Once the direction is set, create quarterly community business reviews and tie them in with line manager and HR partner reviews. Success is hosting an accountability review like the one shown in Figure 6–7, where senior leaders will be able to determine whether or not performance of those in critical roles is improving or not improving.

## Conclusion

A friend who works in finance at a major airline said it well: "Our only variable costs are jet fuel and people, and there is not a lot we can do about controlling the price of jet fuel." In the airline industry, as in many other industries, business success requires a disciplined approach to improving the performance of people. This chapter provided a simple roadmap to that end.

The roadmap begins by building clarifying roles and responsibilities: a GM who insists on a balanced approach to management, a senior leadership team that assumes the primary leadership role for driving year-over-year improvements in organizational capabilities, and an HR function that assumes the role of day-to-day organization-wide change leader.

The SLT is accountable for crafting an HCS that produces sustained competitive advantage. The HCS includes two work streams:

(1) aligning all employees to the business strategy, and (2) systematically improving performance of those in critical roles.

There is a lot to think about when making this fundamental change in the management of human capital. However, start with a grade of B. Those who try to start with a grade of A often never start. Get to an A through continual improvement. Remember that the first PalmPilots were Ds at best.

## Note

1.   J. Rockart, "Chief Executives Define Their Own Data Needs," *Harvard Business Review* (March-April 1979).

# Index